Self Improvement

A Guide to Personal Growth and Development

(A Comprehensive Guide to Personal Growth and Self-improvement)

Norman Turner

Published By **Chris David**

Norman Turner

Self Improvement: A Guide to Personal Growth and Development (A Comprehensive Guide to Personal Growth and Self-improvement)

ISBN 978-1-998038-04-6

No part of this guidebook shall be reproduced in any form without permission in writing from the publisher except in the case of brief quotations embodied in critical articles or reviews.

Legal & Disclaimer

Table Of Contents

Chapter 1: The Confident Introvert: Far from an Oxymoron

A guide to turning into a surprisingly confident introvert, stereotype be damned.

right proper right here is little as terrifying as being called as much as do an unprepared stand-up comedy regular with in some unspecified time in the future's note at the equal time as you're not even a stand-up comedian.

And you're an introvert.

I'd been requested to be tremendous guy at a friend's wedding ceremony. The actual superb man had cancelled, and I became the first-rate friend who prepared the in shape which had already arrived. It became the very subsequent day.

"You don't must do a speech, genuinely maintain the hoop," he said, nicely aware about my introversion.

"I'll do a speech," I responded, and jotted down a few thoughts that night.

I'm British, and in case you're not from proper here you may not understand that the terrific guy's speech is the conventional highlight of the day, apart from the 'I do' factor.

The concept is to tear into the groom and get the entire wedding ceremony guffawing. It's like doing stand-up comedy, however with a selected butt of all of the jokes. Risky is right. I've recounted many human beings to reveal down the feature due to the strain and fears of this immoderate-pressure 2d. In fact, I changed into later informed that the opposite fantastic man had additionally cancelled due to nerves approximately the speech.

The wedding ceremony went nicely however at the reception I realised that my planned speech became a piece too risky and will not pass down properly in any respect. That's honestly simply one of our advantages of being introverts and sensitive human beings; we will experience a draw back-fest a mile off. So, I threw my notes in the bin. Best men who ruin weddings by using going too an prolonged way are not remembered fondly.

Speech time came. The room went quiet. There's continuously huge anticipation for the extremely good guy's speech. Everyone turn out to be smiling, ready for the comedy.

I had now not some thing.

Nothing the least bit, but my introverted mind and my quiet, monotone introverted voice.

I stood up, and people giggled with a bit of luck.

"Hello," I stated. "I'm the brand new great man." The room went sincerely silent, and my introvert brain modified into very aware that every ultimate eye in that room modified into on me.

"Is absolutely everyone prepared?

Because I'm no longer."

The assumption for such lots of is that introversion through a few technique equals shyness, and that introverts, through their very nature, aren't confident.

I'm right right right here to tell you otherwise, and I'm here to inform you a manner to do it.

If you're not seeking to acquire the now not feasible and come to be an extrovert, and as an opportunity desire to come to be quite confident for your actual self, you're within the right vicinity. This is the mind-set we introverts should take.

Just test out any typical overall performance video of introverts Elton John, Lady Gaga or Robbie Williams. Introverts can be especially confident. But it doesn't usually need to be in that form of way. These men are performers. They find it irresistible. You may be that confident in doing some thing you want too.

If Rosa Parks didn't have the braveness to refuse to surrender her seat on the bus to a white man, racial segregation would have lengthy past on for even longer than it did. She have become an introvert with the courage to stand up for what modified into right — and changed American and international records.

Just watch Emma Watson or Nelson Mandela communicate. They're introverts, however they're alternatively confident.

Being quite confident as an introvert is really viable. It can take some paintings but first it takes a few expertise.

"The day I commenced out to live is the day I located being an introvert grow to be exceptional."– Maxime Lagacé

There's this big misunderstanding in society that introverts are usually shy, and that shy people are mechanically now not confident.

There are issues with those instead pervasive assumptions. Firstly, self warranty can be very a bargain contingent on context – a shy character in one state of affairs may be extremely confident in every specific – and secondly, introversion and shyness are not the identical issue and in plenty of processes aren't even associated. They really frequently look the identical at the floor.

This motives every distinctive hassle, in that introverts sense that a few issue is come what may additionally incorrect with them, and that sample of concept can harm self guarantee. The reality is that there's in fact now not a few thing wrong with being an introvert, and it comes with benefits surely as extroversion does. It's clearly extrovert advantages are very seen and introvert advantages are greater diffused and internal. But they're very lots there.

Shyness and its pathological big brother social anxiety are not just like introversion.

Whereas shyness is a worry of being judged with the beneficial aid of others, introversion is extra to do with sensitivity to social stimulation and our need for quiet relaxation. If we get overstimulated socially then we also can feel uncomfortable and get worn-out, even into the next day with what's known as an introvert hangover.

Extroverts, meanwhile, want more social stimulation to avoid boredom. In on the lookout for that stimulation, they'll be loud and chatty and sing and dance and behave in all of the strategies that society imagines confident human beings behaving.

But self perception isn't a behaviour. It's a experience and a belief in ourselves. If others mistake our introversion for shyness, that's on them. It doesn't alternate the internal feeling, mind-set and self-notion that is self perception. And we introverts can revel in that self guarantee too.

A loss of self belief or low conceitedness is due to horrible ideals approximately ourselves. Because society is so fixated on the extrovert ideal, we're vulnerable to questioning that due to the reality we don't in shape that 'first-rate' photograph, and due to the fact looking for to behave that way makes us experience uncomfortable, that there's a few component incorrect with us. Feeling and questioning that there may be some component wrong with us isn't the road to self warranty. We want to reject society's extrovert ideal.

Extroverts have sure advantages for positive – but so will we. There's nothing incorrect with being an introvert any more than there's a few factor wrong with being left-handed. Society is installation for one manner, however the precise manner brings blessings too. Left-handed human beings need to cope with painful scissors and smudged pens, but they're additionally higher on common at sports activities activities and maths.

We need to deal with society praising the extrovert perfect and adults telling greater youthful introverts to attempt to be extra extroverted and feeling like our way isn't as right. But we're even though much more likely to advantage achievement CEO's.

Ignore society's extrovert exceptional, or like left-handers with scissors and the entirety else designed for manual use, discover ways to get with the useful resource of with it just great. But understand, and I will say this masses because of the truth the arena desires to realise it, that there may be not a few aspect the least bit incorrect with introversion.

There's now not something wrong with being shy each. Some people are, some human beings aren't. But if you don't like being shy, you have were given were given the choice to paintings on letting it pass. This is not an opportunity with introversion.

The key to self notion as an introvert is this: You do not want to be confident in all of the situations an extrovert is. You do no longer want to be assured being a noisy and large person.

You quality want to be confident in doing the property you want to do, and assured sufficient to mention no to the rest.

And but, as continuously, it's now not quite that simple.

Confidence growth occurs in big element outdoor your consolation location. Being an introvert is a cute way to live, but it shouldn't be an excuse to live to your comfort region and no longer increase.

It's genuinely, genuinely essential to recognize the distinction among shyness and introversion. You can paintings to reduce shyness through way of growing your comfort quarter. You can't reduce introversion as it's deep-seated in your character and in component in your DNA.

Untangling the shyness from introversion and then embracing the introversion is a completely vital step. Social tension may also additionally require professional remedy, however a few strategies on this ebook may moreover moreover assist too.

One of the matters we introverts are proper at is introspection, and this will are available very beneficial. We observe internal topics due to the truth we're not chasing extra out of doors stimulation, and if we get over-stimulated socially, we note the ache. We're used to noticing those gadgets. Especially if we're as an alternative touchy, which many introverts are.

Noticing feelings is important, however expertise a way to respond to them is critical. What is self guarantee, if it's no longer our capacity to do what we need regardless of the soreness? Confident humans although enjoy nerves. They simply act regardless.

For some motive, we always think our emotions are proper. Always correct. Always to be acted on if viable. But regularly feelings are furnished through the primitive components of our mind that aren't even logical, so why are we able to constantly suppose they're mechanically correct?

Take the ones examples:

I'm indignant, you need to apologise!

He pulled out in the the front of me and indignant me, he need to clearly have his license taken away!

Luckily, we don't continually reply to our emotions within the manner they endorse. Society is probably horrible if we did. Punching without a doubt everybody who makes us angry isn't always socially perfect but a good buy we might revel in adore it every now and then. We simply allow society's pointers override them and begrudgingly behave efficiently. Yet even as we get our introverted feelings, we certainly obey in location of overriding them, and might get caught in our comfort-zones.

If we supply commonplace revel in into play, matters can look particular. We all make errors the use of. That using pressure who lessen you up can be out of vicinity and harassed and experience horrible for the error. That intimidating female is probably irritating and putting on a courageous face however overcompensating. But our emotion centres don't think like that. They simply reply fast with an emotion and we honestly assume they'll be correct and justified.

But what if we were to assume in a distinct manner approximately our emotions, which incorporates the feelings that consist of introversion? What if we are able to trade how we reply to them? I endorse this:

Feelings aren't something however an invite to bear in mind taking action.

They're not anything more. They don't have the intelligence potential for additonal. They don't manage us and we don't should manage them. They're really invites.

Sometimes you may need to gain this. Feelings come for a cause and sometimes they will be right. But act on it with the aid of considering its invitation and taking over that invitation, in place of blindly letting it manipulate you. Bring well judgment into play and see if the feeling is logical, like you could with the cause force who made the damaging mistake.

As introverts, we might get feelings of pain in or on the danger of heavy social stimulation. But feelings don't control us. They will invite us to move home or live quiet or flip down an invite – however we don't need to do as they may be saying.

Stop seeing introvert social pain as all-powerful. It does now not control you. Start seeing it as a mere invitation on a flimsy piece of paper. Let logical questioning assist you solution the invitation.

As introverts, at the same time as social stimulation receives above our consolation threshold, we start to revel in uncomfortable.

This ache is what we occasionally mistake for shyness. With a keen introspective thoughts and a few exercising, you'll speedy determine the two.

An introvert who isn't shy may though experience this soreness. We're being bodily overstimulated at the neural and thoughts chemical level, notwithstanding the whole thing.

What is this soreness? It's a enjoy. And what are feelings?

Nothing but an invitation to keep in mind taking movement. That motion may be going domestic. Or it is able to be going to the bar for pics to 'medicate' your introversion for the night time time. You may be given or flip down the invitation to act. The movement you pick out is as an lousy lot as you.

There's not anything incorrect with introversion and it doesn't want medicating. But there's additionally nothing wrong with ingesting and dancing all night time time too if that's what you enjoy. You'll have a hangover the next day from the booze though, and we introverts can also have an introvert hangover, too.

That uncomfortable, socially overstimulated introvert feeling modified into what got here upon me as I stood in the the front of the two hundred marriage ceremony visitors ready to supply a speech I hadn't written. And the action I determined to take, have become to snort. And then the sensation out of place its power.

In improvisational comedy and clowning, there's this idea that there's no longer anything funnier than seeing an actor 'in the sh*t.' That's a technical time period in clowning.

This approach that the actor is installed a position wherein there aren't any options left, they haven't any concept what to do or wherein to go with the scenario, and the target audience is privy to that the actor is in that horrible scenario too. As the pain leaks out of the actor desperately operating out how to get out of the sh*t, the target market laps it up. We love searching improv actors squirm. It's hilarious. Long-taking walks TV display Impractical Jokers has made a phenomenon out of it. The entire display is the guys putting each special within the sh*t over and over another time, we watch them squirm, and it's one of the funniest suggests on TV.

And there I become, an introvert referred to as to first rate man obligations the day before and having surely thrown all my notes inside the bin. I end up maximum honestly in the sh*t.

Because I'm an actor, I knew a way to play this and made awesome they knew I became inside the sh*t. If I become a charismatic extrovert, I can also need to have virtually talked my way out of it. But I'm not. I'm an introvert. So I used that to make the pile of sh*t I modified into in even massive — and that made it all the funnier to take a look at.

Because I wasn't in truth scared — that is approximately being assured in your introversion regardless of everything — I made positive to interrupt a real smile from time to time surely to permit every person understand I become good enough in reality and they didn't need to revel in uncomfortable too. I achieved the characteristic of the 'introvert in the sh*t' and they cherished it.

By telling them that I had a speech that had without a doubt lengthy long gone inside the bin because it have come to be beside the element, I have become allowing them to understand I even have come to be squirming. I didn't try and supply a classically great speech. I didn't try to act more extroverted. I permit them to recognize I become in trouble, and allow my introversion do the relaxation.

They cherished every 2nd of it. So did I. Two instructed me it changed into the exceptional wedding ceremony speech they'd ever seen. Three asked me if I grow to be a standup comedian. The end quit result were a 'deadpan' comic normal which were given a laugh each time I test a line off the wedding itinerary. I had no speech notes (I actually have grow to be inside the sh*t) and that turn out to be the closest thing to be had to take its area.

Incidentally, I later instructed the particular jokes in non-public to the groom who thanked me for now not sticking to that script. It ought to now not have lengthy beyond down properly in any respect.

I permit you to recognize all this not to relive the honour of that speech, but to reveal you what may be very viable at the same time as making a decision to come to be confident on your introversion in preference to questioning that self assurance equates to extroversion. You can end up a totally confident introvert with that smooth alternate in thinking.

Simple and smooth aren't continuously the same factor of route, however with a piece of try, it's very workable.

Whatever is going on inside the introverted mind of yours in a social state of affairs, you'll be surely accurate sufficient with it. Any awkwardness, whilst you prevent taking it extensively, can actually end up a laugh. That's wherein self notion lies.

Untangling the shyness from the introversion is something that each one introverts can do. Then are you able to no longer handiest luckily acquire being an introvert, however clearly revel in it and all the advantages it brings. Shyness may be reduced or removed with the aid of the usage of consolation-area stretching and one of a kind techniques you'll discover on the approaching pages. Cured, if you want. But in no way try to remedy your introversion. It can't be performed and if it could, you'd be dropping an excellent a part of who you are.

What you're left with after the shyness has long long gone are uncomfortable feelings introduced up thru more social stimulation than you're comfortable with. This can be in a noisy club, busy examine room, or perhaps simply due to the reality you're assembly a stranger. It may be due to the fact you're in an introvert hangover and it received't need masses stimulation the least bit to feel uncomfortable till you're rested.

But the ones emotions of ache, those overstimulation feelings, are just an invite to accomplish that. Feel loose to take the invitation, or to say no it. Accept it and positioned your self within the sh*t for comedy effect in case you need. If you discover it funny too it received't make things awkward. It'll make topics humorous. People love parents which might be the on foot oxymoron of snug in their private awkwardness.

We may additionally additionally see an entire lot of the advantages of extroversion and need we had them – however that's most effective due to the fact extroverted advantages are at the ground and there for all to appearance. Our blessings are inner but beautiful and we shouldn't want to lose them for the area. If it's self belief it's far the extroverted trait we respect and preference, then it's self notion we are capable of get. But in our very very own introverted manner. And that doesn't should mean being loud, chatty and right with strangers.

It method being suitable with ourselves. It manner being satisfactory with the fact we get uncomfortable. That's only a feeling, notwithstanding the whole lot. Just an invite. When we be given that, it loses its electricity.

It approach being extremely good with our introvert hangovers. It approach being nice with on occasion saying no to social gatherings. Saying no to a event may come upon as shy, however who cares? If you don't need to transport, say a assured no thank you. Shyness should without a doubt reason you to say certain in spite of the truth that you don't want to due to the fact you're concerned approximately being judged for pronouncing no.

So say no. Or say certain. Say you'll determine closer the time. Say anything you virtually want to mention. That's what assured people do.

Here's a few other acting term which is available in useful:

Public solitude.

Public solitude is being by myself, but in public. Drinking a espresso by myself in a espresso store, going to a cinema by myself, even dancing on my own in a nightclub.

A shy character generally doesn't like public solitude. They'd be worried about being judged for being on my own. Maybe for having no buddies. But a confident introvert will embody it. If we like to people-watch, then we'll visit a coffee save and do this. If we need to see a film alone, we'll try this. It doesn't depend range what others assume.

Seek out public solitude. If there's any shyness spherical it, it'll speedy go away. It's a quick and smooth step in the direction of being a assured introvert. You like being by myself — so get confident being on my own in public. Go to a espresso shop, sit down by myself, positioned your cellphone away, and experience the espresso. You're by myself, and we're glad on my own. There truly happens to be wonderful human beings spherical too.

Text Box: Public solitude is also a outstanding first step to untangling shyness from introversion. You can sit down down in that espresso shop by myself and screen any emotions of ache. Are they because of the reality you're concerned humans are judging you (shyness) or do you not care approximately that but if it gets busy and loud you begin to get a touch uncomfortable (introvert overstimulation)?

On the situation of being judged, it's not surely wonderful humans that could determine us. They not regularly do. More frequently, it's what we do to ourselves.

It's very critical to trade the way you decide yourself to your introversion. If you pick out your self badly for now not being as accurate as an extrovert in social situations, then that's not wholesome. Be kind to yourself.

Notice things you'd need to artwork on of course, but do it without judgement. We're introverts and we get uncomfortable and worn-out spherical too many people. That's truely first rate. No bad judgement is needed.

If there's some aspect precise you need to work on due to your profession preference, or due to the reality you revel in some thing that isn't a incredible in form for introversion, you can art work on that in particular and your thoughts will adapt.

If you're shy, doing this will assist with that too. As I said before, shyness is also context-based.

When I did the pleasant guy speech, I changed into but quite shy in some of tactics. But I became confident in public speakme – at the identical time as a shy introvert. This end up because I'd been in that feature numerous instances in advance than and triumph over shyness in that context. Firstly, I completed in a band so was used to having eyes on me, after which I become an actor, so I even have grow to be used to talking inside the front of people. I'd studied comedy concept so I knew the manner to play it. I emerge as confident in that excessive context lengthy in advance than I have become confident in others.

This is a extremely good example of procedures we're psychologically bendy. Shyness isn't always constant. Our individual modifies over time relying on what we do and the conditions we emerge as in, or placed ourselves in. My as soon as degree-shy individual now loves it.

It's furthermore beneficial to bring in what is known as narrative identity: the recollections we tell ourselves approximately who we're. If we inform ourselves we're quiet and shy and typically can be, then that story sticks. If we determine that's now not a part of our identity and we as an alternative inform ourselves we like to spend lifestyles outdoor our consolation location, and then start to live that tale, our individual will trade to in shape the tale. And then we'll honestly do this, and we are able to develop.

If you come to be confident in the context of a normally extrovert-area which include public speaking, then you could anticipate emotions of overstimulation even as you do it (genuinely invitations) and additionally an introvert hangover. That's all top notch. Accept it and stay with it. A large a part of self perception is accepting topics about you that aren't ideal and being certainly suitable sufficient with it.

But turning into highly assured as an introvert can take a few greater work. Becoming unique at some thing takes a few paintings. Extroverts have it fortunate on this manner – as they're searching for extra social stimulation they get used to one of a type situations and their consolation zones amplify, often important to extroverts becoming naturally assured as a derivative of being extroverted. Lucky them.

Confidence in social situations doesn't come as a spinoff of being introverted. We can end up confident in ourselves and in our introversion and therefore assured humans, but self notion and shyness may be context-based, and there might be contexts wherein we want to push ourselves if we choice to grow to be confident in the ones domain names. It's additionally in reality extraordinary to optimistically flip down possibilities to be in the ones situations – however attempt to best if you turn them down due to the truth they don't appeal to you, not because of the truth you're scared.

In certainly one of a kind phrases, do what you need. Like a confident individual.

It's adequate for social conditions now not to appeal to you. It is probably good enough and really regular for public speakme to now not attraction to you. It changed into smooth for me due to the reality I've worked on that place mainly for my paintings as an actor and musician.

So pinpoint the areas of your existence you want to be especially assured in, and paintings on it. Learn approximately it and get obtainable and do it. Put in the work. Don't decide your self for being uncomfortable. Praise your self for doing it except. In time, you'll turn out to be assured within the ones regions. Shyness will evaporate away and feelings of overstimulation becomes effortlessly treated.

In areas of your existence that make you uncomfortable and do not hobby you, you don't want to do it. Just say a confident no to it. If someone asks you to, you may with a bit of luck say no because of the truth it might make you enjoy uncomfortable. Do the stuff you want. Don't do the stuff you don't want to. And understand that that's absolutely excellent.

For some humans with social anxiety and exquisite deep-seated problems, therapy or special assist may be required. There are a few situations a exquisite way to constantly be a barrier to self guarantee, and remedy is probably the incredible choice. There are also self-help remedy alternatives that may be effective, and you could find a few inside the coming chapters.

This ebook is ready converting your ideals round introversion and yourself and making the connection that introversion and self assurance can paintings exquisite collectively and be a part of every unique. If you have got limiting beliefs approximately this which you absolutely can't shift, I particularly recommend seeing a therapist in CBT, IFS or try hypnotherapy.

There are also certain effective breakthrough treatment plans using psychedelics which is probably frequently presently illegal, however which I used to top notch impact.

If you do count on you need remedy, you may additionally artwork on becoming assured in your introversion at the same time. You don't should wait.

As you examine via the following listing, it should turn out to be very obvious, if it hasn't already, that introverts may be particularly confident. This ebook will help to cement this manner of questioning, and you may get extra assured for it.

•Shyness and introversion aren't the same thing, however acting comparable on the out of doors. Separate the two and embody the introverted factor of your persona.

•Understand that self notion is context-dependant and also you don't want to be appreciably assured in all areas of life. No one definitely is.

•Understand that self warranty isn't a behaviour. It's a enjoy and a belief in your self. You can be confident and not be a noisy, massive person. Quiet self belief is truely extremely good too.

•You handiest want to be confident in doing the stuff you want to do, and confident sufficient to say no to the relaxation.

•As introverts, we are able to get overstimulated thru social conditions and experience uncomfortable and get worn-out. That's simply how it is. It's like being left or proper-handed. There's not whatever incorrect with it. Our benefits come some area else.

•When you understand the proper nature of introversion, you'll apprehend it's now not a lousy issue at all and springs with many benefits. You have no need to choose your feelings negatively.

•Feelings aren't some thing but an invitation to act. You can pick out out the way to act, or pick out out to decline the invitation, however do it consciously.

•If you're ever in a social situation and locate your self 'inside the sh*t,' realize that it's honestly humorous. You can snigger on the situation too. You're adding loads to the state of affairs via permitting it and accepting it instead of on foot away and feeling lousy approximately it. There's no longer anything funnier than someone 'within the sh*t,' and getting comfortable and confident collectively along side your personal awkwardness is rare and pretty endearing.

Chapter 2: How to Find Your Courage After Growing Up Shy

Shyness doesn't have to be all of the time

Grew up shy Worse, in truth; I grew up with awful social tension. I wouldn't even get on a bus or ask a stranger the time.

Shyness isn't a eternal fixture of a individual notwithstanding the fact that, and for the purpose that then I've accomplished on diploma inside the front of hundreds, been on TV and taught acting to university university students, and cherished every minute of it. I've left shyness inside the beyond.

Some of my pals had been shy, too. Quiet children have a propensity to combine with quiet kids. Some are nevertheless shy, even though now not as a high-quality deal as they used to be. Others aren't. Some have long past completely the alternative manner. One have emerge as a relationship train. One is now a semi-famous musician. One is one of the maximum-paid supermodels within the international.

Growing up shy doesn't ought to propose shy all of the time.

Get out of the house

Staying at domestic doesn't assist with shyness. It doesn't matter how many books you take a look at on self warranty, in case you don't get out of the residence and mingle with humans, no longer some thing will change.

Worse, now and again if we examine and understand a few problem, it'll offer us the impact of exchange. Sometimes it could deliver us a real feeling that we've changed, and that feeling continues us coming once more for extra. Staying within the residence. With no longer some aspect certainly changing.

People who triumph over shyness get out of the house to look some thing they want to appearance, to play their favored game, or to are seeking out a latest shop for that expert cooking element. Whatever the motive, leaving the house is clearly key to overcoming shyness.

*If you're so shy you can't leave the house, you nearly genuinely have a phobia that would use assist from a therapist. You can begin remedy on line through video or phone name.

Try new matters

If you do the identical topics for all time, no longer some thing will alternate. My twiglet pal attempted all sorts of matters. Eventually, someone supplied a modelling competition and the relaxation is records. My musician buddy said high-quality to an acting function and is now on Netflix and well beyond his shy time.

These are excessive examples for tremendous, but what in the event that they'd said no to the whole thing? What inside the occasion that they'd allow their shyness maintain them of their shy container? They may nicely despite the fact that be there. New subjects motive new feelings. One of these will ultimately be self belief.

Old shy people frequently in no way allow themselves attempt new subjects, and in no way changed. How many shy human beings have you ever met who've travelled the world, or completed a whole list of numerous and captivating things? Keep trying new subjects, and the shyness acquired't be capable of maintain up.

Know what you like

Shyness, as self belief, can be context unique. Someone who considers themselves shy may be very confident in first-rate conditions. Just have a check performer Robbie Williams on level – a self-proclaimed shy guy offstage however an all-time superb performer as quick as he steps on. Why? Because he loves it.

"I'm an introvert, and I do an affect of an extrovert. My herbal manner of residing would be sort of keeping apart faraway from human beings, and feeling uncomfortable in social situations."— Robbie Williams

You can see the same in venture, especially in more more youthful gamers. They'll be loud and competitive on the field, however within the put up-in shape interview come over as very shy. How do they overcome it at the pitch? They like it.

When you're doing a little factor you want, all your interest is on that detail and there's none left for your inner emotions of shyness.

It's even been demonstrated through studies that introverts will obviously show extroverted trends once they're engaged in a actual passion.

Then even as you discover braveness and strength in a single problem, it could begin to ripple out into terrific areas of your lifestyles. If you don't understand wherein to start in dropping your shyness, there's no higher location to begin than by way of doing the topics you like maximum.

Push via your shyness

Shyness doesn't go away all via itself. It can appear to – if we're so wrapped up in an hobby because we're loving it, but also keeps us slightly outdoor our comfort region, it'd seem to disappear. But it have come to be absolutely due to the truth we have been out doing that detail, out of doors our consolation area.

That's additionally why shyness can seem to clearly subside as we come to be older.

But if it doesn't appear like happening, or taking location rapid sufficient, we will hasten it on the aspect of the aid of pushing via the priority. When we do things we're fearful of frequently enough, we're not afraid of them.

The first ever time I went on level became a small open mic night time time to do songs as a duo. I drank almost half of a bottle of Jack Daniels in reality to find the braveness. A few hundred gigs later, sober, and I even have end up absolutely bored of playing. I felt now not something the least bit, least of all fear or shyness. I'd driven through my fears and acquired. I moreover forestall music due to the fact I changed into bored. It grew to turn out to be out I desired the concern problem extra than the bass gambling.

People who grow up shy find out their self assurance by means of way of doing the very subjects that scare them.

Accept and understand your introversion

Remember, introversion and shyness are not the identical thing. Shyness is to do with a worry of judgement from others and a lack of self belief to position your self beforehand in social situations. Introversion is a want for quiet by myself time to relaxation and being absolutely overstimulated in social conditions.

However, human beings conflate them all of the time. Shyness is a trait most humans don't want, and if shyness is conflated with introversion, then it follows that introversion is a trait we don't need, or a few thing to be constant, or worse, be embarrassed about. It's not. Not not no longer.

Introversion is a adorable way to live with many, many benefits. If you're ashamed of it and seeking to restore it, now not anything will trade. You can't change some thing that's component genetic.

But if you encompass and love your introversion and work to your shyness – they're separate matters despite everything – you then certainly definately'll be lots more confident in your self.

People who boom up shy and discover self notion, if they're an introvert, encompass their introversion and all that includes it.

Allow self belief to boom immediately from quietness

The element about quiet and shy human beings is they'll regularly select to stay at domestic rather than going out to socially scary sports activities, however non-horrifying others might in all likelihood see it.

We don't circulate domestic and sit and stare at the wall. We perform a little component. We do it hundreds. Then we get properly at it. We have more time to get proper at this stuff than individuals who spend masses of time socialising.

What takes area to those gadgets? They turn out to be passions and immoderate competencies. When we're skilful at something, we sense confident in doing it. When we're operating on our passions? The same.

That trait of being quiet and shy grows proper right into a capacity of passion, and that grows into self warranty.

Lose the disgrace of being shy

A massive compounding hassle with shyness is that we assume if we're shy there have to be some aspect incorrect with us. Then we sense disgrace approximately our shyness and withdraw into our shells. That's how shyness breeds more shyness in ourselves.

But what if we dropped the shame? What if we realised that shyness is a completely everyday a part of human nature. There's not anything incorrect with it. We can remove it if we want over the years, or take shipping of that we're a bit shy and that's in reality ok and normal. What happens then?

Then we prevent chickening out into our shyness and start to put on it on our sleeves. That's not an area wherein shyness prospers, and it begins to vanish away.

All human beings have some shape of trait they don't assume is right. Some are lazy. Some are clumsy. Some conflict to understand standards others discover easy. Some are shy. It's all a part of being human. There's no longer something incorrect with it. Shyness is even a trait that might make you greater likeable. Once we prevent feeling bad approximately being shy, it loosens its grip.

People who conquer shyness save you demanding that they're taken into consideration shy.

As we alternate, so do our brains

The reason this stuff art work and that we're no longer tied to our shyness all the time is in a big element because of a way referred to as neuroplasticity. That's wherein our brains shape new neural pathways as we do new subjects. If we preserve doing those new topics they get less complicated. If we in no way do the antique matters, the vintage pathways close to up.

So in case you're shy and constantly using those shy neural pathways, they'll stick. If you preserve doing new subjects, you'll forge new neural pathways so as to in the end get much less tough to use, after which become the latest you. The a superb deal less you experience shy, the greater the ones antique neural pathways will become redundant and the feelings of shyness will reduce.

That's the technical era aspect. Then there's this: Confidence modified into continually there, deep down. Have you ever visible a shy toddler, or do they scream and shout the residence down once they need a few factor? It's the second, normally. At some factor on your lifestyles, you located to be shy. That technique you may unlearn it.

You may be sensitive to overstimulation of social conditions, some factor notably tied to introversion, however that's fine. You may be assured in that. Own it. The more you observe your self, the more you can be comfortable in yourself.

Shyness doesn't should be all of the time.

If you have got got social anxiety, you may want a touch greater assist. That's what therapists are for, and a whole load of on-line belongings. Social anxiety doesn't need to be all the time both. Mine wasn't, and mine end up terrible.

Try new subjects. Embrace your introversion. Cultivate your abilties. Push through that shyness. Forget approximately any idea of shame of being shy. Forge new neural pathways. And especially, get out of the house.

Chapter 3: Goodbye, Social Nerves

Tried and tested techniques to be an awful lot lots less apprehensive socially

One day in the course of my socially disturbing years, I became reputation in a file save, looking to pressure myself to talk to three other patron. I'd promised myself I might speak to at least one stranger that day and the plan grow to be to in truth ask for the time. I'd in no manner controlled to try this earlier than.

But tension took over. My toes wouldn't budge. I located my dry mouth clamping spherical my tongue. I had no risk. Talking to strangers clearly wasn't viable for me then. Some a part of my thoughts might also need to bolt my toes to the floor and gag me till it have end up strong.

It took me a few years to recover from that. Today, I'll talk to all of us. Socializing with strangers have end up possible and, now, finally smooth.

I completed this partially through residing out of my comfort place, mainly thru strolling as an actor. Psychology and treatment qualifications additionally helped, and prepare, the consequences were as extremely good as I need to have dreamed of. And now I can pass at the stuff that worked the incredible.

If you battle with social nerves, proper here's a manner to get beyond them.

Try 'consolation-region stretching,' however make it slight

Comfort-region stretching changed into a normal a part of my lifestyles for decades. Similar to CBT's immersion therapy, it's common advice because it works.

But the important component proper right here seems to be a nicely-saved thriller: in region of the image of leaping from an plane to stretch ourselves, it's often higher to genuinely lean gently out of our consolation zones. Little however regularly so we don't get too terrified and skip backwards. There's not some thing to be obtained through way of almost traumatizing ourselves.

So anything diploma you're at, in reality look to push out a piece in addition. It may be asking the stranger the time in case you've were given social tension as terrible as I did. It might be telling a shaggy dog tale to a cashier. If you've made masses of improvement already, it is probably as a protracted way as improv or stand-up magnificence—but don't revel in you need to do that until you revel in (almost) equipped.

The hardest element I did, even beyond improv instructions and solo visiting, have become stroll right into a McDonald's and order a pizza, in essential phrases to look stupid. My line after being told they don't sell pizza end up "I'm sorry, is this now not a Chinese eating place?" It have become genuinely terrifying.

Don't begin there, however in case you're prepared to perform a little issue totally nerve-wracking, I advise it. Normal social conditions will in no way feel scary once more in comparison to that. That's the power of comfort-quarter stretching.

But don't overlook to exercising self-reputation, too

Self-popularity is big in conquering social nerves. Sometimes staying on your comfort region and know-how there's not something wrong with that is truely what you need. Here's why:

Part of the purpose we revel in horrible approximately being socially concerned is we think it shouldn't arise. We see so many thankfully extroverted humans, beneficial strategies like consolation-vicinity stretching, and assured people at the TV, that we begin to suppose that if we experience worried, there's a few aspect incorrect with us. There's not.

Social nerves show up to quite a few people. It doesn't devalue you or propose there's a few thing incorrect with you. It's certainly that every one humans have a few topics that make us uncomfortable, and that's considered one of yours. Nerves are a everyday part of being a human.

So in area of having pissed off approximately feeling awkward, if we are able to without a doubt take delivery of that's how human beings from time to time are and are aware of it's definitely appropriate sufficient, we are capable of get snug with it. And then, ironically, we'll gain the self belief to be more social because of the reality we're extra confident in ourselves.

So take shipping of that's how you're for now like such a lot of others, and realize it's adequate to be that manner. Go out and stretch your comfort vicinity, too, however don't fear if on occasion it doesn't exercising session. I failed limitless times and it became all part of the manner. If you get too hectic and don't be successful, it doesn't imply there's something wrong with you. It's handiest a being human issue.

Take the highlight off your self

The issue approximately nerves is they're an internal feeling, and to preserve any strength the least bit, they want your interest. They do attempt difficult to seize that hobby, however you don't should permit them to be triumphant.

There's a right way and a difficult manner about this. If you try to resist or forget about about about your nerves, they'll shout louder. They'll nag and phone you till you offer in, and that enables no character. There's a higher manner.

You have finite hobby to give. So in region of attempting no longer to offer any to your nerves and function them shout louder, alternatively, supply it all to three component else. If one hundred% of your attention is on a few issue else, then there's 0% left in your nerves.

What's the excellent area to vicinity this hobby on? No, not your phone! The awesome person. They'll love you for it. It takes some exercise, but it truly works a enchantment.

In appearing, we use some factor known as the Meisner Technique wherein we teach to area our hobby absolutely on our scene partners. It's like going to the gymnasium, but for interest. When doing the wearing activities, the whole lot else seems to disappear away. The faces searching, the room we're in, and sure, our nerves. All the eye is on that amazing person.

In those sports, we're inside the front of an goal market and our nerves want to be at their maximum, but they're now not, because of the fact there's no interest for them. It works like magic.

Research permits this idea, too, finding that people whose interest become interior stated greater anxiety in social situations, and regarded more annoying too. The look at furthermore positioned that socially traumatic people often did this habitually, so if that's you, get that interest on the outdoor.

Break eye contact on the identical time as you need to of path (otherwise it's absolutely weird), however otherwise, offer your interest to your pals, date, or maybe strangers. Just not your nerves, and they'll lose their electricity.

Blur the road amongst nerves and pride

Nervous emotions are, at their middle, a bodily reaction of chemicals like adrenaline being released into our systems. This sends our thoughts a signal, and our brains fill within the facts with a manner to interpret it. If we're in a state of affairs we'd count on to be worried, we'll interpret the ones emotions as aggravating.

When we're excited, it's the same. The equal chemical substances, the equal middle feeling, however adjusted with the resource of the translation of the thoughts into pride.

This manner that, on the fundamental degree of a physical reaction, nerves and satisfaction are the identical element. The difference is your interpretation of it. There's top notch information right proper right here: we will switch the two round. No greater nerves, truly delight.

How can we do this? The system is known as cognitive reappraisal and actually includes telling ourselves a way to revel in. Use phrases like "I'm excited" or "This is thrilling" or commands like "Feel excited." Keep doing it every time you're frightened. Eventually it'll paintings, possibly pretty abruptly, and nervousness will become excitement.

You'll still be scared while you need to be – if you're being mugged there's no need to tell your self you're passionate about it. This is exactly how I had been given over my degree fright and feature taught it to acting university university students with superb consequences, too. More on this springing up.

Try hypnotherapy

Here's some other angle of attack you can do by myself as frequently as you need.

Hypnotherapy is largely approximately becoming very comfortable, after which the use of your creativeness or recuperation memories on the identical time as our defenses are down. You don't need a therapist to do that. There's a totally easy approach you may use which follows those standards, that you could use at home by myself inside the consolation of your private bed.

It's a two-stage, repeated technique. One diploma is to get very relaxed. The specific is to visualise a scenario that brings up the nerves — possibly an interview, date or public speaking — and then as you feel the anxiety arrive, right away pass once more to the rest method. That manner you train your thoughts that in location of a frightened response, the state of affairs will provide you with a relaxed one. Clever, eh?

There are many rest strategies you could use. You can use hypnotherapy style guided visualisations, respiration techniques, frame scans and hundreds more. Use some difficulty works extremely good for you. Whatever receives you surely, deeply cushty. If you are sudden with the techniques, surely are seeking them on Youtube and you can find out a few audio to guide you.

Then while you're in fact cushty together together with your eyes closed, consider your self entering into that scenario that makes you concerned. Make the pix amazing and practical so the nerves in truth begin to arrive — and then right now get once more to fun. Repeat as commonly as you need to.

You can use soft, tool lyric-unfastened track in case you need. Each time you do it, your intellectual pics will come up with a good deal a whole lot less of a apprehensive feeling, and this need to translate to the real global. It's a shape of mental rehearsal — leaving your consolation zone without even leaving your bed.

Just don't handiest do that, and fall into the entice of doing this in region of going out into the real worldwide. This is a manner to conquer social nerves — no longer avoid them!

Change your language to and approximately yourself

If you talk over with your self as a shy or nervous character, then that's now not going to help subjects exchange. It may be cementing it as part of your identity.

It's not always going to paintings concerning your self as assured both, due to the fact in case you finally don't revel in confident, you will likely sense cheating, or dissatisfied and irritated. That's why I keep away from affirmations. They can revel in like improvement at the same time as there's none in reality there, and moments that undertaking the affirmations can experience like a backward step.

So the primary aspect is not to use language about yourself like shy, involved, quiet, or related phrases. The subsequent is to avoid absolute terms that can be proved incorrect, like "I am continuously assured" or "I in no manner get apprehensive".

Chapter 4: Nice climate in recent times isn't it?

Yeah, if you're a duck.

I 'm British, and in case you spend a whole lot time outside the house here, you'll pay interest that shape of trouble plenty. We do love to say the weather.

Because I'm so hyper-privy to those little matters as a few introverts are, it'd make me balk each time a person said it. I should in no way dream of doing it. Better to live silent, the introverted and socially worrying factors of my brain ought to agree.

A lot of human beings locate such small speak excruciatingly awkward. But the problem is, while we watch two humans have interaction in the ones monstrously useless exchanges, we then watch them have a right verbal exchange, and wonder why we are able to't do this. Maybe they'll end up friends. And it all commenced with a stupid declaration about the weather.

Here's the way to make all of it a hint much less complex.

Recognise the dance

Eventually I found out that there's nothing incorrect with small talk. It's a part of the human conversation dance, the first step ahead. You can see what the alternative character is like, or within the temper for, before doing anything that topics. Yes it's obvious waffle, however it's obvious waffle that human beings acquire and expect. If they solution in a disinterested way, you've lost no longer some thing.

Think of it just like the first step of the dance. The first little leap forward. Nice weather nowadays, isn't it? They'll get hold of the invitation and dance with you ('Lovely, and despite the whole thing that rain' or different such nonsense), or will allow you to understand in their private manner they don't want to bounce. If so, you've out of location virtually no longer something.

If you strive and begin a communique with some aspect you accept as true with you studied is witty and unique and that they're no longer concerned, then you may experience rejected. That's a private issue. You've finished a massive dance flow and nobody joined in and also you enjoy silly. Small communicate is a manner to look in the occasion that they're inside the mood in advance than you offer them that chance.

It's the first step to look inside the occasion that they want to step with you. It's the provide of a chance for them to show disinterest without it being personal. Shutting down small communicate isn't shutting you down, it's displaying that now isn't an super time, or they're shy themselves.

It's a first rate, herbal a part of the human communication method and no longer something to be awkward about.

Lower your requirements

The lower the same vintage of the hole the small talk line, in plenty of ways, the better. The more lame and forgettable the outlet line, the a superb deal much less non-public it is if they're now not inquisitive about a talk.

That's in element why we've got desired traces like speaking approximately the weather. It's mundane, however each person can relate. It additionally doesn't take each person off guard and feels herbal, even though a number of us flinch at it. It's a doorway. You don't go to a residence and hate the truth you want to open the door. You simply open it. That's what small speak is. The proper stuff is the opposite facet of the door.

People who're sensitive to human subtleties can word what's taking place and flinch. Socially worrying human beings might imagine they want to say some thing profitable or in no way. But the alternative is actual – say what you need, however mundane.

You're truely starting the door. It's simply giving them the opportunity to subtly allow you to apprehend in the event that they want to talk.

Don't fear approximately what comes subsequent

Worrying about what to mention next is commonplace. But even as you're deliberately reducing your standards, what's there to worry approximately? If you are saying some difficulty a piece garbage, that's the purpose. People care quite little. Either you'll get on well and stuff will examine glaringly, in any other case you received't and it received't do not forget. If you have got intentionally low standards you received't worry about hitting them. If you via using hazard say some issue smart or witty or make them smile then high-quality. But that's no longer the goal.

If the character you're talking to isn't a person you're definitely in passing with and you actively want to take the conversation similarly — in all likelihood you're networking or hoping to get a date — then there are masses of smooth little verbal exchange tips coming in a while to assist maintain subjects easy.

The one large cause

It's not pretty an entire lot starting a door and seeing if you every want to transport in addition. If you'll in no way see the man or woman once more, then small speak however has a characteristic, and it's a large purpose why we do it: to lead them to feel comfortable.

Some human beings don't like silences. Some people get demanding round people they don't understand. By without a doubt pronouncing a few issue dull and mundane but unthreatening, you'll cause them to revel in comfortable. They'll realise you aren't going to be competitive or weird. That's the issue approximately stupid and mundane setting out lines. They're now not bizarre, and that's all you want to make a person feel cushty.

It's the not understanding someone that makes people awkward. Using popular small speak is a way to allow them to recognize you most effective a tiny bit — and revel in greater comfortable.

The big goal then is virtually to show you're no longer weird or aggressive. Beyond that, it's clearly supplying the first foot and seeing in the event that they're up for a talk, with now not some thing misplaced within the event that they don't. It doesn't sincerely bear in mind.

If you revel in the alternative person isn't even up for small communicate, then you could simply live quiet too. It's not vital and silence is honestly fine.

If you don't want to either then that's also exceptional. There's no longer some component incorrect with that (in any other case you). Just be comfortable in the silence in choice to awkward because of the truth you determined you have to destroy it. There's no want if you don't want to.

Keep it easy, hold it smooth

Smalltalk might also need to make some humans which include the socially demanding or touchy draw back up, however frequently the benefits of an top notch chat or perhaps a modern day pal or courting are without a doubt the alternative component of those preliminary moments.

I want to admit I in no way point out the climate because it although makes me balk, but I not thoughts while people say it to me. I see it for what it's miles — an invite to expose I'm up for a chat, or a manner to in a polite manner and subtly say no thank you. Because that's all it is. I'm grateful for the invite. I'm grateful they took the first step.

For a six-foot large man, it's a fantastic way to expose I'm not intimidating too.

Just do not forget:

1.Understand that small speak is there to serve a simple motive and open the door, or offer step one. It's a way to see if they're inside the mood for a chat without a actual chance of rejection.

2.Keep your requirements low. This gets rid of the stress of how you may come over and is all part of the dance. Just be aware some component mildly exciting spherical you and point out it.

three.Don't fear about what's subsequent. Just pay attention and have a look at what takes region. Make a touch upon some aspect they'll be pronouncing, and hold those necessities low. Once the door is open, you'll realize in case you need to preserve the chat going. Or maybe you'll have entertained a few bored employee for a few minutes. Either manner, you've misplaced now not something.

Chapter 5: Stop Caring About Little Embarrassments

The 'highlight effect' fools us into wondering all and sundry sees our little moments

Imodified into onstage under lighting, gambling bass and keyboard in a 10-piece band in the front of three hundred university college students, with snot putting off my chin.

I'd sneezed, and it hadn't long past well. Snotty mucus clung to my mouth and dangled from my lips. I ought to enjoy it swinging. With both my hands busy gambling the bass, I became caught on level and now not the use of a opportunity but to cowl.

Crouching down inside the once more of my keyboard for some cowl, I grew to come to be to our violinist, who burst into disgusted laughter. With some hammer-on (one-handed) gambling, I managed to type of clean myself up with my spare hand. But everything had played out on a stage inside the front of masses.

You realise what? No one found.

Luckily we were a 10-piece band and I wasn't the singer, which honestly helped, however this had took place to me at the identical time as I changed into absolutely on a diploma beneath the lighting fixtures, and however no one located.

People see our little embarrassing moments a long way a whole lot less than we apprehend. The cause we get self-acutely aware about the smallest of factors is due to a highbrow trouble called the Spotlight Effect.

Next time you're taking walks thru the street and revel in self-acutely privy to a few factor, take self notion from the truth that in all chance, no character cares – or may even likely be aware. Here's why.

The Spotlight Effect

The Spotlight Effect is called such because of the truth we supply ourselves the affect that we stroll spherical with a spotlight on us, and absolutely everyone's hobby is interested by us at the same time as we make even the slightest mistake. That little adventure at the concrete crack, that small brown mark on the equal time as we sat on a grimy wall, even though we're wearing an embarrassing novelty tie a few extrovert gave us as a present. In our heads, really anyone sees.

But they don't. Very few humans observe, an awful lot much less care. When we realize that, we can in reality begin to use it to our benefit.

The motive for this, as psychologist Nathan Heflick perfectly places it, is that we're the centre of our own universes, and examine the area spherical us as such. Why don't humans look at the subjects we're so self-aware of? The same motive. They're all the centre in their very own universes too, and are a ways more concerned approximately their very non-public worldwide than anybody else's.

People have issues, hopes and goals, stresses and plans of their very personal, all strolling through their minds. They don't have anything to advantage with the aid of the use of noticing a stranger's novelty tie as they rush thru.

People additionally have their very personal time desk to have a laugh at the equal time as making a song and dancing to a band, or be self-aware in their dancing, or try to trap someone warmth at the dance ground. They don't have time to have a look at the bass player protected in snot putting from his chin.

That's how we escape with almost the whole lot that is probably otherwise embarrassing. Except, because the centre of our personal universes, we persuade ourselves that everybody else noticed too, and we cringe horribly.

Feel plenty less self-aware

The manner to use this to our benefit is pretty easy. Just understand the Spotlight Effect, and remind ourselves of it whenever we're in a characteristic we think genuinely anybody is calling.

"You'll worry much less approximately what people remember you while you recognize how seldom they do."– Olin Miller

Ok, if you're giving a TED talk and also you fall over, all of us is going to look. But in case you're truly residing your existence and do a little factor clumsy, don't worry. Remind your self that the fine one that cares is you. Everyone else has their private little global to worry approximately.

In all risk, no one noticed. Get on collectively together with your day, pull away-loose.

If it is able to paintings for a person with social anxiety on degree with snot on his face, it may be just right for you.

A Simple Thought Switch to Kick Social Nerves

Some more approximately the maximum essential distinction amongst being anxious and excited: your interpretation

Being anxious is a horrible feeling, isn't it? It doesn't need to be.

As an actor who had social anxiety, I understand this better than truly every body. With assist from my psychology records, I found a cognitive cheat I nonetheless use to nowadays.

Nervousness begins offevolved however doesn't give up with biology.

When we get anxious, our bodies launch adrenaline. We get the shakes, butterflies in our stomachs and our hearts beat more difficult. When we get excited? The equal.

Our our our bodies need that combat or flight chemical rush whether or not it's to defend within the route of an interloper (nerves and fear) or to walk out onto the sports activities activities sports area (pleasure). Both situations want our our bodies to beautify themselves to perform – to combat the intruder or knock the ball out the park.

The huge distinction amongst nerves and delight is how we consider the sensations these chemical materials deliver:

•Nervousness is a highbrow interpretation of a bodily sensation.

•Excitement is a one-of-a-kind intellectual interpretation of that identical bodily sensation.

•Nervousness and delight are quite a extraordinary deal the same feeling. The distinction is how we view it.

But what about social nerves?

It's that same physical response once more. Social nerves advanced in us very early, prolonged in advance than we had undertaking interviews and tempo courting. We get demanding now because of the truth whilst early humans tousled socially, it can be bodily dangerous too.

Back then, if the organization you tried to entertain didn't including you and took offence, it may be really existence-threatening. Thinking about drawing close to that lovely cavewoman? What if she's the accomplice of the tribe leader? A possible membership to the pinnacle. What if you humiliated yourself socially and had been given exiled from the tribe? Social mistakes may additionally need to have violent or maybe grave effects. Our bodies replied as although there was a risk of physical risk due to the truth there has been.

We don't have the danger anymore, but we although have the response, and want a way to get it on our issue.

Flipping nerves to pride

If feelings of anxiety and pleasure are the equal problem, and it's only our interpretations which may be wonderful, why can't we simply interpret our social nerves as satisfaction? Then we'd be passionate about our public talking gig or first date or improvised comedy direction. Why can't we attempt this?

The real information is we can.

I discover this technique top notch. As a as soon as-involved actor I needed a few factor like this, or I'd were terrified all the time. It doesn't normally paintings right away, however maintain on repeating the notion method, and shortly enough, worrying will flip to excited.

It's not just me. I occasionally educate show acting at a pinnacle arts college and educate this to my university students. Those who pursue it may't take delivery of as proper with the distinction. No greater degree fright. Just exhilaration to carry out.

Is there any studies on this? Yes. It even has a name in Psychology – cognitive reappraisal – and it's been confirmed to be very powerful. A observe at Harvard determined that "Compared to people who try to relax, people who reappraise their traumatic arousal as excitement sense extra excited and carry out higher."

Flip it

How is it completed? Whenever you're feeling concerned, inform your self you're excited. The greater you do it, the simpler it will probable be. I not often need to do that now and routinely enjoy excited in which my social nerves turned into.

I use labelling to trade my perceived feeling (that is a super instance of CBT's reframing), and say things like "I'm excited" or "This is thrilling". You can also use commands like "Get excited". As lengthy as you're switching your interpretation from 'fearful' to 'excited' it have to artwork, and the more you do it, the higher it receives. As the cognitive behavioural therapy announcing is going: trade the idea; change the feeling.

So that's it. The most effective and simplest method I realise to now not be socially concerned. Tell yourself you're no longer involved in the long run. You're excited. It obtained't be prolonged till you truly are.

Chapter 6: Common Big Mistakes in Beating Social Anxiety

If you're operating on beating social anxiety, here are a few traps to avoid.

It took me ten years to eliminate my social anxiety. Sometimes, it felt like I turned into going backwards. It appears, it's due to the fact I have come to be.

Social tension impacts round 7% of the population (USA statistic), and I had it worse than maximum. I located lots approximately the way to cope with it and finally conquer it – what to do, and what to strive not to do.

Here are the 3 largest mistakes that held me decrease lower back, and plenty of others — which can even make topics worse.

1. Confidence guidelines are not designed to heal a highbrow

state of affairs

When I started to alternate my lifestyles, I didn't understand I had social anxiety. I'd by no means heard of it. I definitely belief I was shy and favored self warranty. So that's what I were given all the manner all the way down to do — emerge as confident — the usage of common self guarantee enhancing strategies.

Some of this works. Confidence hints aren't continuously all that particular to social tension development strategies. They every regularly encompass getting out of our comfort zones and getting a piece a awesome deal lots less frightened whenever. So in concept, this could have labored. But it didn't, and in fact, at times made subjects worse. Here's why.

Confidence enhancing pointers involve things like this:

•Approaching strangers and hanging up a communication.

•Deliberately speaking louder and greater definitely.

•Showing confident body language through using setting up up and spreading out.

This is all properly and correct. However, on the same time as someone with social tension attempts this, the subsequent can show up:

•You see a stranger to approach, panic and once more out.

•You shape up to talk loud and easy but panic and get self-aware and say not some component at all.

•You open up your body language and then spend all of the time traumatic about drawing hobby to your self, and come to be even greater quiet.

This all then leads to a similarly problem.

Because the ones topics seem smooth and without issues practicable, and we fail to obtain them, we are able to then revel in horrific about ourselves, like there's some thing incorrect with us - and then we start to cross backwards.

Trying a few detail so apparently smooth and failing isn't actual for our shallowness or self assure, specially at the same time as we sense so self-conscious as we fail.

What to do alternatively

Confidence techniques may be extremely good, but wait till you're ready. Start more small. If you strive one and don't control it, in vicinity of wondering "I can't do it", assume "That's a few aspect for the destiny."

Once your social tension is lengthy past, and it could take some time (and that's extraordinary sufficient), you'll have all of the time in the global to mess around with these things.

Or, in case you're feeling courageous and decided and experience that they're the right component to do, then bypass proper in advance. Just realise that if it's now not as easy as you idea, in any other case you get surprising setbacks, that's without a doubt good enough and anticipated and a part of the journey. It's not some thing that's incorrect with you. You're brave for trying, not inadequate as it didn't seem right away.

What I may advise to nearly every person, despite the fact that, is organised improvised comedy instructions. These are the scariest topics in the global to a socially disturbing person, and quite terrifying to even the socially confident - but they're based totally in a strong way to permit you to get used to looking stupid in the the the front of people, and realising it's not that horrible ultimately. Long-shape, American fashion is higher for social anxiety than the British brief form one-liners. There's now studies to once more up the idea of improvisation for social anxiety, too.

2. Always being looking out to look what had to be consistent

I'm a glaringly inquisitive and strategic individual, and whilst that want to be an advantage in searching for to methodologically remedy problems, while the trouble have become my tension, it brought on some other mistake.

Because I changed into constantly looking for issues to treatment (it's not just me, human minds are problem seekers and solvers), I targeted on my demanding troubles, and the results of my tension. When I attempted and did now not perform a little factor, I noticed the problems it changed into growing. And then I have grow to be getting disturbing about those issues. Not an excellent restoration.

If you continuously interest to your tension and its difficult signs, that's all you'll see. My anxiety genuinely commenced out to set itself in more potent as I started to discover as a socially disturbing man or woman. This wasn't the purpose in any respect.

As effective additives have been solved, different things have been then determined out to additionally be regular. It changed right into a in no way-completing treadmill of troubles. A conveyer belt of factors incorrect with me. I become specializing in the incorrect element.

As the extraordinary Jordin James says in a tweet;

"You will in no way experience secure to play in case you are constantly on the lookout for what although desires to be constant internal of you."

Although self-awareness and discovery is an crucial part of healing, continuously that specialize in and scanning for issues inner ourselves isn't the way ahead. It's a manner to keep reminding ourselves we're now not but in which we need to be.

What to do alternatively

The secret is to reputation on the property you've finished and also you experience, and then do extra of them.

There are one of a kind gaps in self-development:

•The hole among wherein we are and wherein we need to be.

•The hollow among who we have become as quickly as and the way far we've come.

I consider specializing in the primary hole the most crucial very very own cause in self-development. Focus on the second one, and proper topics begin to show up. And of course, don't forget about to revel in the present.

Get there through taking component in the adventure, not residing on the problems. And, as Jordin's tweet concludes, "Let yourself play."

3. Not accepting that the purpose changed into imperfection all alongside

A huge part of social anxiety is the fear of being judged with the useful resource of manner of others. For no longer being perfect, and having others see that. Even in case you haven't but admitted it to your self, that's very often the reality at the back of the tension.

So my mistake, and a totally not unusual one, is to then attempt to restore everything so it's far best. So everything does degree up. Confident frame language, fun and flowing communication, success in a few factor we do inside the the front of people so we don't appearance silly.

The hassle is that's a purpose we're able to in no manner attain. No one is extraordinary. Trying to beautify yourself so you degree up in every unmarried way is not possible. And so the anxiety in no way is going away, however plenty development we make.

That's not to say there's no charge in getting real at those objects. There truely is. But if you're socially annoying, the anxiety obtained't leave until you're satisfactory, and that day will in no way come so long as you're someone.

What to do as an alternative

If the anxiety is because of fear of being judged for our imperfections, and we are capable of in no way be great, then what are we able to do? We can change the alternative a part of the equation: obtain that it's first-class to be imperfect.

Make it your motive in region of to be pleasant, to be ok with being imperfect — due to the truth all human beings are. Your quirks and imperfections are what make you human. Fiction writers write exactly those imperfections into their characters to cause them to likable. Your imperfections are a top notch element. They make you likeable too. Accept them.

This can be hard to swallow earlier than the whole thing. You might not need to pay hobby it. If you've got social tension and are afraid of being judged for these gadgets, being informed to reveal them to the arena isn't smooth. None of this is meant to be snug and clean. But it's far extraordinary in high-quality techniques.

Understand that you percentage your imperfections with billions of different people everywhere in the international, which encompass celebrities and global leaders. They're a part of you, humans including you for them (in case you truly had been ideal, you'd be silly and unrelatable), and you may't 'repair' they all besides.

So prevent that specialize in fixing what you endure in thoughts to be incorrect, and begin to simply accept them. Self-development works higher with kindness to your self.

After the anxiety

Ultimately, all of the subjects I did to help my social anxiety did help, in spite of the truth that I made some mistakes along the way which held me up.

The self assurance and self-development sporting events can also moreover have helped however ultimately it come to be remedy and psychedelic healing that taken care of my anxiety for suitable. After that, all of the advantages of the self notion paintings shone through, due to the truth I'd located the artwork in and the tension changed into no longer there to keep me decrease once more.

There's a root purpose of social tension, and remedy is the way to cope with that. Meditation also can assist a few too, genuinely a few robust introspection. Self-reputation and self-compassion will assist extra than diving too a long way out of your comfort location and risking feeling lousy as it hasn't worked for you even as it does for others.

Understand that your flaws are what make you human, and you may't be perfect. Accept that, and things gets higher.

Above all, if matters don't workout how or as speedy as you need them to, don't judge yourself for it. It's not approximately beating the social tension via placing apart it and attacking it. It's about being type to your self and it's about play.

Be kind to your self and play.

That's subjects that lets in you to help in existence prolonged beyond the stop of your social anxiety, as and on the identical time as that takes area. Keep being kind, keep gambling, and it'll.

Conversation Tips That Work Like a Charm

Bring more pride in your conversations with small and clean strategies you could have a examine in a direct

You apprehend the ones painfully awkward TV interviews at the same time as children supply a string of one-phrase answers, and you can almost sense the interviewer squirming in desperation to make it even remotely exciting?

That grow to be me, in each communication, nicely beyond my children years. Probably past my teenagers, at instances. I sense for the terrible those who struck up a communique with me. If that's what you may call it.

Anyway. The advantage of being so very crap at a few aspect so very essential manner you need to discover ways to do it. And then you definitely honestly apprehend the manner it without a doubt works. Here's what I determined out.

Say a snug goodbye to awkward silences

I used to have so many awkward silences. Not nice because of the reality I didn't recognize what to say, however moreover because of the truth as a more youthful man or woman the people I mixed with have been moreover more youthful humans, and they didn't understand the way to manage. They felt my awkwardness and iced up up. Double awkward.

But that's the difficulty approximately an inept silence. Almost continuously, it takes . If one man or woman relaxes, so does the alternative. This lets phrases begin to drift yet again, or for all people to be in snug silence collectively.

Interjecting with any vintage rubbish honestly to fill a silence can draw interest to it and feel awkward in itself, although it normally leads once more to conversation so the awkwardness is brief-lived. In that way, it's an preference.

But the manner I love to do it's miles definitely to be cushty within the silence, and display that I'm cushty. That manner the opportunity man or woman will loosen up too.

Conversations ebb and go with the float. They pause certainly at times. Pauses are an component of the conversation cake. They can be as comfortable as you are making them.

Rather than scrabbling around in my head for a manner to restart a communication, or freezing up in awkwardness, now I choose to showcase consolation.

Lean again. Breathe. Notice thrilling subjects spherical you. Unfold your fingers. Sip your drink but do it slowly and revel in it. Slow it down. Find your presence. Make your self comfortable.

Then the other person will observe.

The closer you're to a person, the greater silences will become a part of lifestyles. A couple married for half of a century will take a seat down for plenty minutes gambling each super's enterprise with out saying a phrase. It shows comfort and closeness. Treat silences with new humans as an opportunity to illustrate which you're snug with them.

Comfortable silences may be adorable moments. All you want to do is slow down, open up, and show it.

"There is a few issue rather civilised about permitting prolonged pauses in a communique. Very few humans can stand that shape of silence." –James Robertson

Taking recommendations from adorable birds

Hostage negotiator Chris Voss has the first-class method ever for buying comfortable conversations going and starting up connection. He has to. The conversations are immoderate strain and lives are honestly at stake.

Voss demonstrates this approach in his Masterclass, and it makes use of the easy idea that people are mimicking creatures much like parrots. If we mimic a person in communication, it received't appear bizarre. We're hardwired to definitely receive it. And but it seems too clean to be right.

How can we mimic for easy verbal exchange? By in reality repeating exactly what they said to you, phrase for phrase, for his or her closing three or four terms. If you're ever caught for some factor to mention, simply repeat the previous couple of phrases verbatim, and let them hold their educate of belief.

Not simplest is it suitable for communication, but it receives people to like us too. Researchers tested the idea using equipped body of workers, teaching one organization to answer with such things as "Coming up!" or "Ok!" While the opposite group repeated once more orders word for word.

The surrender result? The parroting waiters obtained 70% better pointers.

We surely are hardwired to mimic. Don't consider me? Try it. No one ever notices.

Make them experience comfortable like a therapist may want to

There's a similar technique to Voss's parroting technique referred to as reflecting, this is used by therapists and counsellors to make humans revel in heard and cushty.

The method consists of repeating once more what the character has certainly said to you, but in desire to phrase for word, paraphrase it.

This demonstrates that you've listened to and understood what have become said. I had a place of job friend as speedy as who did this for ninety% of his conversations, and he became the maximum well-known guy at paintings. I watched him appeal people for years in advance than I eventually worked out what he have become doing.

It appears too obvious, like we'd get busted the use of techniques, but humans don't recognize. People simply find it irresistible, and the folks that do it.

It's a ridiculously smooth element to do, and faucets into our need for being understood and heard. Therapists do it for a reason. And no person will ever comprehend.

Avoid the unintentional accusation

Another issue negotiator Chris Voss desires to do is keep peoples guards down.

Otherwise, he can lose consider and rapport rapid and people can also additionally want to die. So there's a few issue he avoids doing so he doesn't danger that.

According to Voss, most human beings get yelled at as youngsters after a mistake with the word "why?" Why did you damage that? Why did you draw that there? Why did you consume that?

As such, we develop up being a chunk protective spherical why, and it could final all the time.

So in place of asking why in a communique, try to rephrase it. Instead of "Why do you need driving?" strive "What is it approximately the use of you want so much?" The guard stays down and the communique continues flowing.

Add sparkle like actors add chemistry

Despite my shy beginnings, I've been a display actor and occasional trainer at one of the pinnacle arts universities in the u.S.. Teaching this stuff is terrific and attending to see the most effective of stuff art work proper in the front of my eyes can be some issue precise.

Sometimes although, matters may be quite easy yet nonetheless no longer clean. Adding chemistry to a scene – and the perfect same policies practice to verbal exchange – is one in each of this stuff.

Basically, it's done by way of the usage of method of getting your attention mostly on the possibility person. A hundred%. If they do the equal to you, that's wherein chemistry starts. In performing, we use a few element called the Meisner Technique and take a look at this step by step over numerous years. But that's because of the reality actors need to do it intensely for prolonged intervals, again and again, with severa distractions and on the same time as remembering traces. So for an actor, it's like going to the gym.

It's tough in advance than the whole lot, but receives plenty less tough. Like muscle groups inside the fitness center although, it is able to be a case of use it or lose it. Get your interest at the alternative character and hold it there. They'll love you for it.

It need to be obvious then that placing your interest on some thing else doesn't help, till you're moreover directing their attention to it. Having your attention on one aspect even as their interest is on you does no longer purpose accurate verbal exchange.

You can workout a chunk too at domestic on my own with mindfulness techniques to begin constructing the muscle. As short because it becomes smooth, you'll in reality study a difference. And as fast as you be aware that distinction – it technique your interest is back interior. Put it decrease again on them.

It's furthermore a splendid way to lessen social nerves. If your attention is absolutely on the opposite character, then it could't also be for your awkwardness, shyness, nerves, social anxiety or a few component else. All those matters are interior you. Keep your attention clearly out so it has no room to live on the ones subjects which is probably inner.

Make it amusing like comedy improvisors

The reason that comedy improvisers make all of it look so smooth is that they're surely following a load of guidelines that make it seem that manner. Comedy improv is huge amusing and I quite advise taking schooling. It's as hilarious as it's miles to begin with horrifying. You'll in no manner be the equal another time.

But there's one method that's the muse of all of it, it's called 'sure, and.'

Yes, and works in actual lifestyles too, and it's quite easy. Instead of replying with an opinion, rebuttal, associated anecdote or some factor else that comes from inside you, reply through agreeing (the high quality detail) after which one manner or the other building on it in addition (the and).

Conversation can emerge as extraordinarily fun and playful this way. It's no longer in reality for use in debate or immoderate tones, but if you're definitely gambling round or passing the time, it could result in unusual, a laugh and humorous moments.

How to be exciting, defined in terms

There's a commonplace word that short explains the way to be more interesting. It's from Dale Carnegie, writer of How to Win Friends and Influence People:

"To be thrilling, be worried."

Being worried works for some reasons. If you're truely interested, your interest might be on them, and we already apprehend how that could bring about connection.

You'll moreover in all likelihood keep in mind their call, which makes human beings warmth to you.

But the most important aspect may also truly be that it gives the alternative individual a threat to enjoy proper. According to Samantha Boardman M.D.:

"Well, steady with one take a look at, speaking about oneself turns on the same areas of the mind that light up while consuming proper meals, taking tablets or even having sex. Simply located, self-disclosure is exceptional. It offers us a neurological buzz."

People will have a excellent time truely talking to you about themselves. And then after the communication, they'll maintain in mind that that they had a extremely good time and feature that to you. And all you probably did have become be concerned.

"The artwork of verbal exchange lies in listening." –Malcolm Forbes

Go with the go with the flow

Conversation isn't tough. Even if it feels that way, while you realise that every one the air doesn't want to be packed with phrases, it all of sudden receives a tremendous deal less hard.

It's much less difficult but whilst you recognize that you could without a doubt parrot once more or rephrase what they've stated. Not handiest is that smooth, but humans love it. They love it plenty that specialists do it all the time.

You can up the game from essential to a laugh or sparkling verbal exchange via the use of techniques from appearing – keeping your hobby firmly on the opportunity individual and making topics a bit silly using sure, and.

And in case you want them to take into account a splendid time, definitely permit them to talk about themselves.

Lean lower again, breathe, embody the silences and the phrases of the other character, and say some thing yourself. Even if it's precisely what they certainly stated to you. They'll love you for it.

Chapter 7: The Learnable Traits of Charismatic People

Methods from psychology and the arena of appearing will add as a whole lot as the most charismatic model of you

Charisma isn't magic. As an acting train, I train more youthful actors a way to deliver it out in themselves and function chemistry with their scene companions. As a psychology fan and creator, I want to look deeper into the hows and the whys thru technology's eyes.

Here it is, all laid out. What the charismatic do and the manner they do it - so you can get to being a more charismatic you.

They don't conceal internal themselves

Psychologist Richard Wiseman studied air of mystery and decided that one in every of its most vital foundations is being able to surely experience emotion. If you deny that emotion, you're denying your charisma.

We enjoy emotions for a reason. Many reasons, in truth. One of those reasons is conversation. If you bury them, you'll be hiding them no longer quality for yourself but from others. Fully feeling emotion is a big part of charisma. You can't transmit it in case you don't completely feel it your self.

To be charismatic, permit your self to completely revel in your emotions.

They're generous with emotional conversation

Wiseman concluded that no longer nice do charismatic people permit themselves to feel emotion, however moreover explicit it. Avoiding feeling your emotions and fending off showing what you're feeling are various matters, every crucial for air of thriller.

People who show what they're feeling are visible to be extra charismatic, consistent with Wiseman. In education acting, there's an abundance of strategies to get actors to clearly experience emotion and allow it display, in vicinity of just pretending to expose an emotion as recommended inside the script. That's because that's what humans like to examine. That's what we're inquisitive about. That's aura.

We're interested in people feeling actual feelings and displaying them. It can be uncomfortable at the beginning. We inform younger actors to be beneficiant, and show each person what they're feeling. When they allow skip of their insecurities and desire to cover their emotions, their performances come to existence and their air of mystery shines.

To be extra charismatic, don't be afraid to reveal what you're feeling.

They popularity outside themselves

Actors educate, on occasion for years, within the Meisner Technique. It's a very clean factor however takes our talents to an unusually immoderate degree in in reality paying hobby – with all our interest on one-of-a-type humans and not on or in ourselves.

When critics talk about a couple of actors having chemistry, it's now not as mystical as they make out. It's genuinely that those actors have their hobby on every extraordinary virtually and clearly. Not on their very own performing, or their lines of their heads, but on each special. That's chemistry, in a nutshell.

So if you need chemistry and air of secrecy, get your attention at the out of doors. If it's on the outside, there's no hobby left for anxiety or insecurities — they're at the indoors.

Stop thinking about what you must say subsequent, or the way you need to stand, or what to do collectively along with your arms. It'll all cope with itself if you pay attention and watch with all of your hobby.

To be greater charismatic, keep your hobby inside the present 2d on the outdoor.

They keep their arms out from under their bums

Another trouble that's taught inside the Meisner Technique isn't always to sit all the way down to your impulses. Not to muffle your frame language. Not to stifle the little assets you need to do within the very second you want to do it.

We prevent ourselves doing all forms of matters because of our social conditioning and our need now not to carry out a bit component 'incorrect.' We play it stable and sit down on our hands in area of the use of them. There are such a lot of subjects we apprehend we need to do rapidly even as we're free of social conference.

Watch actors free themselves up and act on impulses, and watch their charisma skyrocket. Watch a charismatic character, and you'll see they no longer regularly maintain once more the little impulses they've got. The little matters they want to do, they do without reserve.

Of path, there are a few urges and impulses we should sit down on. In a Meisner elegance it's trustworthy recreation to push, kiss or maybe slap someone if that's the impulse you have were given had been given. Not so in the real worldwide. But you received't with the resource of accident bypass that an prolonged manner. Your thoughts is aware of while to save you you. It's been doing it all your lifestyles. Charismatic people are calibrated in a few other manner and act on the impulses which is probably proper sufficient to do, with little care of looking stupid.

To be more charismatic, act on your little impulses and private them.

They have a exceptional lightness and ease

Lightness. A word with very special meanings, every of which can have a look at to charismatic humans.

They have a lightness of thoughts that consists of a excellent deal a whole lot much less fear. Of path anybody worries, but some humans fear an extended way an awful lot much less approximately what one-of-a-kind human beings assume. These humans can become very charismatic.

This comes with a chunk caveat: Some people may be charismatic because they care lots about what others expect. When people care masses approximately what others anticipate that they qualify as narcissistic, then they'll regularly discover ways to be charismatic out of desperation for approval and reward. But that's now not the proper or healthy way to head approximately topics. It's a ways higher to surely now not care.

How can we pass about that? Comfort area stretching is one manner, looking mildly silly after which realising it's wonderful. Improvisation comedy instructions are exceptional for this and I'll preserve recommending them. They're extremely good for communication capabilities too. Research says it lets in with social anxiety. That's for the above motive – it teaches your thoughts not to care what others expect. You get to appearance silly in a steady, managed surroundings.

There's each other shape of lightness highly charismatic human beings regularly have. That's inside the manner they walk and bypass. They commonly have appropriate posture and walk with their heads held immoderate, and drift lightly instead of trudge. Not always, but it's commonplace. That's a few issue you may examine with appearing techniques from this e book, too.

To be more charismatic, learn how to now not care about what other human beings assume.

They're infectious, in a amazing manner

In the take a look at above, Wiseman located one greater trait of rather charismatic people. Not best do they sense emotion strongly, and show it, however they get different people to revel in that emotion – it's infectious.

This is available in element because of the connection they've got with the human beings they're with – having interest mostly on a person else is how sturdy connections are formed.

Being impulsive, feeling feelings, no longer being worried what others think and being present is infectious, and others round begin to do the equal problem due to subconscious mirroring and reflect neurones firing, causing the emotions to be felt via manner of others.

Wiseman additionally determined that charismatic human beings don't simply have an effect on emotions of others, but don't have their very very own emotions swayed thru the usage of various human beings. They're impervious to the emotional have an effect on of others.

Highly charismatic humans don't absolutely revel in and display emotion, however aren't laid low with other human beings, and get others to experience matters, too.

That charismatic paradox — they don't care approximately being charismatic

Here's a chunk hassle with gaining knowledge of to be charismatic: People who're charismatic generally don't care that they may be, narcissists apart. So with the aid of way of looking to be, your air of mystery dangers a drop. So what are you capable of do approximately that?

Stop being worried approximately this element this is air of secrecy, and begin permitting your self to enjoy the individual additives:

•Let your self experience your feelings and don't muffle them. Emotion is human.

•Let others see that emotion. Emotion is a totally honest form of communique.

•Keep your hobby on the humans you're with and thrilling property you notice, no longer on your head or to your smartphone.

•Let your self be impulsive. Life is extra amusing that manner.

•Learn to stay with the lightness of not being concerned what others expect. You can learn how to stroll with a mild touch, too.

•If you're doing all these items, others may start to sense what you're feeling too. But don't stress it. Just revel in being this way.

The relaxation will appearance after itself. With a piece of time and effort, each person can learn how to be extra charismatic. I've seen it seem in my college students over the route of a couple of minutes, and I've visible some expand it over the weeks and months. Everyone is unique.

But one detail is consistent: if you're thinking about it an excessive amount of, your interest is on your mind – indoors – and sabotaging your charismatic development.

Charisma isn't approximately you. It's about the opportunity humans round.

Chasing and growing air of mystery as a trait is difficult and can be irritating. It's an elusive factor and chasing it superb highlights to us the gap amongst how we want to be and how we are. However, setting apart every thing and on foot on that can be huge a laugh. It's a extremely exciting way to paintings on ourselves.

Enjoy living a bit extra like charismatic people do, in a single particular manner at a time, and air of thriller will follow.

.

FACT

Introverts are often more current. We're satisfied to spend time in our heads on foot out complicated creations whether it's far tune, fiction writing, troubles solving or some element else.

Other People Love Those Things You Hate About Yourself

In screenwriting, we use flaws them to make human beings likeable.

We can spend an extended way too prolonged thinking about our flaws. I spent many years dwelling on mine. Much of the self-help enterprise organisation revolves round assisting us dispose of those flaws (or giving us that phantasm) so we may be happier when they're long gone.

But what within the event that they weren't simply flaws the least bit? What if they come with a plus facet we've in no manner taken into consideration?

What if the topics we hate about ourselves are the same topics that make others like us?

A large lesson from fiction and screenwriting is exactly that. We write characters imperfectly to get readers or audiences on their side. We provide them the bits of you that you don't need to lead them to likeable and relatable. A perfect man or woman is uninteresting. A perfectly superb individual is someone we struggle to relate to. They're cardboard. Perfect cardboard, but cardboard despite the fact that.

You have flaws super because of the truth you're a person or ladies, and frequently human beings like your flaws some distance greater than you do.

The quest to be lots tons much less human

If we may additionally moreover need to take a magic pill in a few unspecified time in the future and wake up with all our flaws lengthy long past, the closing satisfactory man or woman, we'd probably want to transport for it. Wouldn't lifestyles be extraordinary and now not the usage of a nerves or anxiety, no demanding, flying via artwork without a procrastination or tiredness, feeling glad all of the time and with a assured, appealing body language constantly?

Sounds splendid to me.

But believe in case you knew a person like that. Wouldn't they be, nicely, stressful?

How need to we relate to them? What should there be to like?

Ok, we'd like their funniness and sensible communication, and respect them and be interested in them for a bit. And then likely experience a piece inadequate. We may want to in no manner check or relate.

Even Superman has Kryptonite and makes some questionable alternatives. Indiana Jones actually has dodgy morals. Hermione Granger is a snob. If they were too great, they'd be silly to have a observe. You'd have in no manner heard of them.

If we're too ideal, humans can't relate. All people are imperfect. By looking to restore all our flaws, we purpose to be a great deal less human. Which of path, isn't feasible. We can't surpass Superman.

But have a look at how Superman completed Clark Kent, not simply to be disguised, however to be trendy as a actual human. And Clark makes people smile a good deal greater than Superman. That's definitely how we people are, and we love each first rate for it. Even if we don't discover it irresistible in ourselves.

You like your friends because of their unique quirks

Sure, you need them too because of the fact they're remarkable humans and a laugh to be spherical and permit you to while you need it. But that's no longer what makes an exceptional friend. That's the low bar threshold for friendship. If they're not nice to you, you don't like being spherical them and that they wouldn't guide you, then they're possibly no longer a friend.

So after this threshold of fundamental friendship requirements, what makes us warmth to and love our friends?

It's the ridiculous topics they are announcing. The battles they face with braveness whether they win or lose. The jokes they make that handiest they'll, although they're no longer funny.

It's the topics that they themselves may additionally moreover see as cringeworthy flaws. The worrying frame language which you see as uniquely them. Their anxiety you phrase as candy. Their clumsiness that makes you suspect they're hilarious. Their stutter that shows you their energy and strong point.

I've visible it inside the casting room too. When we're casting for a loveable individual, we don't look for awesome-looking actors. We search for some component that seems like people relate to. Often it's most effective a feeling. But it all comes lower lower back to human beings's vulnerability and imperfections. People heat to flaws.

Whatever your weak spot, or anything flaw you're trying to overcome, it might simply be some thing your pals love you for.

Fight for your amazing self but take transport of your flaws on the same time as you have got them

I'm now not saying keep all of the problems you don't like. If it's some component that makes you uncomfortable or is getting within the manner of your goals, then positive, art work on it and beat some thing it is. That can be an incredible experience with rewards and outcomes you'll never recognize till you've achieved it.

But in the period in-between, recollect how we fiction writers create likeable characters. We deliver them the topics which you're in search of to eliminate. You may additionally experience uncomfortable, however it may draw others to you. The proper humans. People who obtained't decide, but will love you for it. That will will will let you loosen up and take transport of them a piece greater at the same time as you have got them.

Your friends are very keen on you, flaws and all. Beat them on your non-public time, on the equal time as you're prepared. Or take transport of them, or become keen on them, like your friends are.

Keep combating for your satisfactory self, however there's no want to revel in uncomfortable about your flaws whilst you do.

If I changed into your creator, I'd have written the ones flaws for a cause.

Chapter 8: Feel More Confident Just with the useful resource of Changing Your Walk

Techniques from acting and psychology assist you appearance and enjoy more confident

People can spot faux self belief a mile away. It's no longer a great look. You need to carry it from interior.

Luckily, there are some super techniques we are capable of borrow from the region of appearing to get a confident look certainly through way of changing how we stroll.

Research suggests how adopting assured body language can motive actual feelings of self guarantee and a laugh, so not only will you look confident doing this, however revel in it too.

First, right here's the manner to make a fool of yourself with body language

One of my preferred stories approximately the British Conservative birthday party is that a few years within the beyond they took a few frame language recommendation that backfired superbly.

Basically, they would stand looking awkward however with a "strength pose" leg feature to try to venture energy — however as an opportunity regarded absolutely ridiculous and became well-mocked during the us. Think comically exaggerated superhero, however with middle-aged posh people in fits. Just searching for "Tory large leg stance" for some ridiculous real-life photos. The Times newspaper mentioned it due to the fact the "pose of the right plonker."

Anyway, you get the idea. You can't constantly in reality duplicate physical body language idea and paste it onto your self. There's extra at play, and people aren't so without problem deceived. Confidence comes from interior.

Feeling assured and being safe

First impressions are extraordinarily critical. Dates, mission interviews, or perhaps everywhere you don't want to experience disturbing are all super places to use this.

I used it loads as quickly as I began walking as a nightclub bouncer. That's a undertaking wherein searching worried can in fact get human beings harm. But if you challenge self assurance and authority (the uniform without a doubt does masses of the artwork), then humans will probable pay interest and each person may be secure.

Walking via a dodgy neighbourhood after dark? Walk via with self assure and don't look like a capability sufferer. Buying a used car? Walk into the dealership not looking like a walkover. Nervous arriving at an interview or date? This has have been given you blanketed.

There are as many locations you can use this as you could consider — nearly any time you enter a room or make an approach with any importance, or just for amusing — and it truly works on every occasion.

I once did this with a class of college students and asked one if she felt absolutely extra assured inside the course of the enjoy. "Ten instances more," changed into the respond.

How to walk with a chunk of fulfillment: Two techniques

Confidence can are available in special seems. The   that I'll supply an cause behind as a way to cowl most human beings and situations are; self-assured confidence (the type I used running the doors), and a graceful self guarantee, on the way to in form a few person types higher. Many women pick out this too, however certainly anybody is precise.

One uses a technique called the Doppelgänger, and uses a clean visualisation. One uses a few component similar to the Yat Method of acting, a touch recognized method that a few stars are skilled in. Tom Hardy is one. This method makes use of language and its clean establishments. Choose the approach that feels right for you, or try them every.

For a self-confident confident walk: The Doppelgänger Method

This technique consists of a clean visualisation and whole internal attention. You'll want to be somewhere you can walk spherical to workout. The acting technique is little-mentioned and exceptional for display close to-usaas it's so natural – so concentrate up actors, too.

You can do it in a massive room at home, out of doors in a park, or simply get right away into it in the road.

Step 1: Create your Doppelgänger

As you walk, accept as true with a ball of heat moderate on your stomach. Let it slowly amplify as you stroll, growing down your legs, into your chest, your fingers after which up into your head. Take some time.

Your doppelgänger of imagined slight will then inhabit your whole body. It'll be exactly the identical length as you. It'll circulate which includes you. If it wandered off by myself, it might be truely recognisable as you from your stature, stroll, and frame language.

Spend a tremendous short while on foot along side your interest in this inner doppelgänger. Get used to switching it off and returning to your everyday manner of being, and bringing him/her once more into you on name for. The quicker you could summon the doppelgänger and allow it completely inhabit you, the extra useful it'll be.

Step 2: Understand which you do nothing and the Doppelgänger does the whole thing

The key to each those techniques is you don't attempt to do something. The British Conservative celebration tried to do, and everybody laughed. People can spot you doing. They obtained't phrase you being, because of the fact they'll just expect it's how you're.

So give up any notion which you're going to genuinely do something bodily. All you're going to do is keep in mind – and remember tough.

Step three: Let the Doppelgänger do the art work

Step three is wherein the magic takes place, as long as you've located the paintings in the first steps, and were given completely familiar together together with your imagined doppelgänger of mild.

As you walk, maintain your imagination and recognition completely for your doppelgänger. Then bear in mind it developing. Growing taller. Wider. Its shoulders widening and its head slowly engaging in better. Keep going until it's as tall as a house and as big as a car is prolonged. Superhero stature and posture. Even larger in case you desire.

Remember no longer to do. Don't try to pressure it. If you try to pressure it and stroll down the street like a superhero, you'll appearance ridiculous. That's doing. If you without a doubt popularity on your doppelgänger developing and doing that even though, it'll come obviously from internal.

Your body will react as a end result. You'll get up straighter possibly with out realising. Your shoulders will widen. You'll undertake a posture of self belief, and bypass as such. And all as in case you're now not even trying.

And the splendid bit is emotions of self assurance will observe. It's the fastest way I recognize to straight away feelings of self belief that affects your frame and mind. Once you're nicely practised, you'll have the capability to call on the doppelgänger in a 2d.

For a graceful, confident walk

Sometimes you might not need to risk looking so dominant, however however appearance assured. You can be a big intimidating man and no longer need to make yourself look large. You may additionally preference to walk greater like a moderate-footed dancer.

For that, the Yat method is quality. It too is based on visualisations, however additionally easy language. Here's how.

Step 1: The helium balloon

The helium balloon is an initial crutch to train you the way your creativeness can exchange your walk. As you stroll, in fact believe a string coming out the very pinnacle of your head, with a huge helium balloon pulling it right away up.

Don't try and stand straighter. Again, the concept isn't always to do something. Just focus on the imaginary balloon and string pulling your head up. See the way it feels, and be conscious how it can change more than actually your neck and determination, but in some human beings, muscular tissues proper all of the manner down to the ankles.

Play with it. Experience it. Don't try and do a little component, and actually don't try to capture your mirrored image everywhere. You're no longer seeking out out of doors comments. Just to construct that imagination-to-frame link.

Step 2: Float and flow

You can permit the balloon circulate for now. You get it decrease returned later.

Now it's time to broaden a sense of lightness. We do this with language, using the terms flow or go with the glide. They're one-of-a-type terms with incredible effects. If English isn't your nearby language, discover the nearest translations you could and strive them as nicely. Different phrases artwork remarkable for unique humans.

As an example, we'll use flow.

As you stroll, recollect the phrase glide and all its meanings. A aircraft glides softly with its engine off. A wheel glides without difficulty along a well-greased rail. Think how smooth gliding is for birds. Keep announcing the word.

Imagine (another time, don't do) your hands out to the thing like a huge glider's wings. If you are making a turn, recall how a glider does that, lightly tilting because it goes. Absolutely the whole lot approximately it is clean and clean.

Practice for a couple of minutes, allowing (not forcing) your body to through some way waft as you stroll.

Then strive the equal with go with the go along with the flow. It's a extraordinary feeling. Feel the distinction and pick out what fits you best.

Step three: Bring decrease returned the balloon

When you're properly practised with gliding or floating, deliver again the balloon. This will pull your head up immoderate however in a gentle and comfortable way. If you're gliding with imagined glider wings, that'll open up your shoulders, too.

Practice for some time. Try great phrases if you could reflect onconsideration on any. In the Yat method we use punch, which offers a naturally aggressive movement from inside. You possibly gained't need to try this in real lifestyles, but it indicates how flexible it's miles and the way you may pick out the phrases that be just right for you. You might also moreover like to apply press, in case you need to appearance assertive, even though I can also endorse the doppelgänger could likely art work fine for that. Still, all people is unique.

The greater you do it, the much less hard it will become and also you'll be able to turn into it on call for.

Don't 'Do', Limitations of the method, and one very last tip

These strategies will make you display self belief from internal, and no individual will question it. Both techniques, especially the doppelgänger, also can bring about emotions of self warranty. Ten times greater, if you be aware of my scholar. There's no need to do. Just use your creativeness, and awareness on it certainly.

I used it masses as an actor on show display, to transport how the man or woman may want to glide without looking like I'm "acting". But you could use them anywhere. Even if you've had been given no purpose, every now and then it's pleasant simply to stroll via the city searching and feeling a whole load greater confident than the commonplace day.

These techniques do have a problem, and that's that they preserve your interest completely inside. That's now not beneficial for having a communication.

But those are although valuable strategies. If you're entering into a room on my own and want to make an have an effect on, they're nice. If you're annoying in a crowd, it's perfect. Hot stranger decided you as you're buying? Now what you could do that requires no questioning. If you're feeling down and need to transport for a stroll and experience high-quality approximately your self, it may paintings for that too.

Research says you get little or no time to make a primary have an impact on that can be difficult to change. Walk into the room searching and feeling confident, and you've gained half of the warfare.

Yes, it's quick self warranty, but enough quick self assure teaches the brain it's stable to be confident. Confidence is generally situation and context-specific except. I'm confident on a diploma in the the front of one thousand humans or breaking apart a fight, however not so much within the the front of a stranger on a Zoom name or in a rustic wherein I can't communicate the language. We can use strategies like this to carry extra self perception into our lives in regions in which we assume we lack it.

One final tip: preserve your eyes off the ground. Keep them at the horizon or above, otherwise you risk signalling low self warranty. But moreover from time to time take a look at for canine turds.

Feeling assured is heaps a good deal less amusing with a shitty shoe.

With a bit of workout, you'll be able to call the strategies up on name for in an without delay. Spend enough time doing it, and your body will select up a modern assured walk as a addiction and it'll become ingrained to your new stroll. And of direction, it could be fun.

Enjoy your new stroll, or even more so, enjoy the feeling of self assurance that incorporates it.

FACT

In a bit environment this isn't always fixated at the extrovert ideal, introverts thrive.

Chapter 9: Getting Around the Problem of Self-Improvement's Biggest Own Goal

The hollow between who we are and who we purpose to be simplest highlights our insufficient feelings. There's a better manner.

Tright here's some element I see plenty in humans looking for to enhance themselves. Something I fell for too that may derail us continuously in our missions to beautify. But in seeing the trouble in myself and others, I moreover in the long run observed a manner round it. It's labored for me ever considering the truth that, every time.

Here's the hassle

When we're striving to better ourselves, there's something we're so frequently painfully privy to:

We're no longer up to standard however. We can't however do the difficulty that we see others doing, the element that we want for you to do, or experience, or no longer experience. We're now not however at our excursion spot self.

This opens up a stressful hole among who we are now and who we want to be. We apprehend who we need to be, and then see we don't however degree up — which consist of to the very problem that we're seeking to remedy via enhancing ourselves. That gap interprets internal as "I'm not applicable sufficient." It highlights our perceived inadequacies. It's the largest, maximum everyday very own cause I see in self-improvement.

What's the answer?

How can we attempt for improvement with out feeling that annoying hole the various fantastic man or woman we need to be and who we are now? Here's a easy, empowering, and effective way around it:

Be a proud paintings in development.

A proud art work in development is development with out the pain. You can nevertheless see your intention new self, but you'll no longer degree your modern-day-day self in opposition to it, and as a cease end result, experience disappointed. A paintings in development isn't completed yet so mistakes and stumbles may be predicted and not unusual. They turn out to be studying reviews. Then we can use them to get higher.

Because a loss of self notion emerge as my awareness, however the reality that I changed into enhancing, I in no way felt assured. There come to be a confident model of me I believed I may be however I genuinely by no means measured up, however a lot improvement I made. There have become continuously that disturbing hole. Then in the future I made the transfer and the entirety changed.

I emerge as now evaluating myself with wherein I'd come from, and now not wherein I was hoping to be. I'd been focussing on the wrong hollow. Compared to in which I'd started, the distance changed into large! Confidence breeds self guarantee and improvement speeded up. I now not have social tension or self assurance problems. I'm in spite of the fact that not exceptional, however desirable day, I'm a proud paintings in progress in order that's quality.

Try it. Start seeing yourself as a chunk in development, and be pleased with the truth. Next time you get rejected, or experience insufficient or fail, you'll experience the difference. In the center of failure, tell your self you're a proud paintings in improvement and that this is certainly part of the manner. When I do that, I can in reality experience my shoulders lighten up. My identity is not a person who needs to decorate. It's an identity of a proud paintings in development who's come thus far, and even though going. That brings a sense of self perception in itself. It pulls the threshold right out of rejection, too.

It's the distinction among being the shy individual at the birthday celebration kicking themselves for being too shy to have amusing and that same man or woman relishing in how masses amusing they could have now as compared to in advance than.

Self-compassion

It's a form of immediately self-forgiveness, too. It's a part of self-compassion, this is excellent for highbrow fitness. It's a manner of telling your self that the entirety is right, despite the fact that it's now not going perfectly. A art work in improvement is, thru the use of definition, now not going to be perfect and that's clearly good enough. It's a form of what CBT calls a cognitive reframe, one in each of remedy's nice features.

By labelling yourself a proud paintings in development, you preserve it framed in the high-quality. You're no longer most effective a piece in improvement, you're a proud paintings in improvement, and also you're nailing it, via all the americaand downs. It's a highbrow highlighter for all of the progress you've made.

The element is, you're a chunk in progress whether or not or no longer you want to be or not. Nobody's the finished, ideal human. It's a reality. You would probable as nicely proudly acquire it and body it to your advantage. Then you enjoy like you could take on the region, due to the fact you recognize it gained't hurt in case you try to fail. Finished products fail in the event that they don't degree up. A work in development learns and grows higher.

Everyone takes time to development. All humans alive have horrific and off days. All human beings are messy, make illogical alternatives and reduce to rubble. Absolutely no person is right. So in your journey as a proud paintings in development, on the identical time as you lessen to rubble, and you may because of the reality everyone do, you could take the brink out of it via the use of reminding yourself that each one people reduce to rubble — it's a part of being human. You're really doing what humans do. It's a much less painful part of existence for the proud art work in improvement.

This can be the unmarried maximum impactful change I've made to my questioning. There's no pressure anymore. I don't want to live as an lousy lot as being in reality pinnacle at a few element — and that takes the strain off and we might also need to me do my super work and function fun doing it. A tiny slither of unhappiness replaces what turned into crushing. I can take knock-backs and flow on with a grin. I'm no longer substandard as compared to what I need to be. I don't have a few element impossible to live as much as. I'm focusing at the right hollow and seeing how some distance I've come, no longer how a protracted way I have to pass.

I'm a proud paintings in improvement, and I locate it irresistible.

Reclaim Your Innate Confidence Through the Evolutionary Story of Your Ancestors

Time to educate your internal caveman it's secure to go away the cave

Wbird I had remedy for social anxiety, I became fortunate enough that my therapist changed into additionally the pinnacle of a huge, forward-thinking remedy affiliation. He's extremely passionate about remedy and truely as informed. Even as someone who is aware of plenty about treatment, he used smart techniques I'd in no manner heard of.

Of course, I needed to look it all up, and analyze the thoughts and strategies for myself. I can't help it. Which approach you get to pay hobby the ones mind too and use them to your non-public lives, without the pretty huge hourly price.

One of the mind he used combined evolutionary psychology with metaphor to provide an purpose of and reframe any instances I regarded to take a backward step. You also can use it to help waft in advance, and locate the self belief that changed into in you all along.

Caveman psychology is our psychology

It's no longer simply the obvious loss of technology, small dwelling agencies and exciting style options that make our eras so one-of-a-type. We lived a bargain greater like animals then. Fighting like animals wouldn't were unusual. Fighting with animals wouldn't either. Every time we left our cave, there could have been functionality hazard. Danger at ranges now not like anything we've have been given now. Ok, they wouldn't have needed to worry approximately weapons or crossing roads, however pretty a whole lot the whole thing else might've been greater unstable. Even the subjects they used for food or garb can also at instances have fought once more with enamel and claws.

This is in component how we evolved right into a mixture of introverts and extroverts. A simplification: While the extroverted left to get additives, the introverted historical human beings should have stayed home inside the caves. This makes feel for survival. A one hundred% introverted network staying in a cave and not trying to depart isn't going to prosper. But if a hundred% of the network left and were given butchered via a few distinct tribe, there wouldn't had been everybody left both. Having a mixture of the two made feel.

A simplification perhaps, but it's actual sufficient to create the tale that we're capable of use to enhance ourselves. It's a easy visual picture that makes enjoy. What honestly happened all of the ones centuries inside the beyond doesn't absolutely rely range for us as humans searching for to enhance ourselves now.

But the middle fact is that this: staying inside the cave became an entire lot more stable than to transport away it. The risk out of doors might absolute confidence have delivered on a number of them becoming pretty annoying about leaving. To stay home become to stay consistent. The human beings demanding approximately leaving the cave could probably have had a higher danger to stay on — and bypass on their genes to you. We're bred to be worried.

But we also advanced with the resource of manner of being assured. The courageous had been given available and had been given the meals, beat the opposition and surpassed on their genes. The self belief that took on the dangerous forests and animals and marauding tribes – that self guarantee were given passed down the chain to us, too. The self warranty indoors you is a end result of every considered one in each of your ancestors having it in them.

When a cave isn't most effective a cave

The thing approximately caves and the protection they provide is it doesn't sincerely exercise to actual caves. It applies to all kinds of matters. It applies to analogies just like the consolation region. It's moreover a tremendous, beneficial metaphor, and metaphors may be surprisingly beneficial at the same time as we need to exchange ourselves.

"Metaphors sincerely trade the manner we recollect a concept on an subconscious degree." — Psychologist Melissa Burkley, Ph. D.

Metaphors provide us some issue to latch onto. They can provide us steerage in the form of easy-to-observe memories. They've been applied in treatment options like CBT and hypnotherapy considering Milton Erikson used them in 1935 and possibly earlier than. You also can need to argue it's been due to the reality the Bible and one-of-a-kind holy books, and in all likelihood earlier than then, too. Maybe they're as vintage due to the reality the cave-dwellers this very metaphor is based totally totally on. They go through due to the reality they paintings.

Modern cave-leaving situations

Whenever we want to leave a scenario and input every distinctive one, we might also additionally get apprehensive. Got a present day undertaking? It's regular to be concerned. Playing recreation at a brand new, better degree? It's ordinary to be involved and may in truth be unstable. Moving to a current city or united states? Again. Nervous.

Why? Because a few deep a part of our mind wants to positioned us off doing it. Remember, we're bred to be fearful. The very reality that we're still alive technique anything we've been doing so far has worked. That's pretty masses the primary purpose of our brains. So on the same time as we want to do some aspect else, that a part of our thoughts chargeable for preserving us alive devices. After a while of doing it, the brand new thing acquired't make us annoying anymore, as those elements of our brains see and take shipping of that the modern-day difficulty is regular, too. We get desensitized to life out of doors the cave.

Comfort zones are our modern-day-day caves

This is exactly why comfort place stretching works. We educate our brains grade by grade that doing new subjects is steady. Our brains are biologically almost identical to our historic ancestors, and people brains advanced to cope with huge angry animals in place of angry bosses or idiots commenting on the net. But they respond the identical way because it's all they recognize.

So for you to train the ones ancient components of our brains that we're secure, we want to do new matters for lengthy enough that they may research that the brand new topics are good enough. You can't inform a caveman mind that getting a activity as a teacher is secure. It doesn't recognize what a trainer is. So you want to reveal, and allow it observe step by step. That's precisely how comfort area stretching and exposure remedy works — and publicity remedy is one of the excellent remedies we've were given. As we do the ones subjects, the cave metaphor may be extraordinarily beneficial. It helps us visually and virtually understand and song what's occurring, and it allows us comprehend that we're responding as absolutely everyone do and there's not anything wrong with us.

The cave-dweller in you

We're all cave-dwellers inside the personal vintage elements of our brains. The cave is steady. It's heat and there's no wolves or snakes. Everyone indoors is part of a protective tribe. The elders looked after you and taken you up. The others feed you and also you feed them. You're a set. It's an first rate location to be.

But outside the cave? Possible danger. This is why while we stretch our comfort vicinity, and it's higher to lean out step by step. First peer out of the cave for lengthy enough to revel in worried, then flow back internal and sit down down thru way of the fireplace. The subsequent time, you can take a step out. That's an entire lot better than leaving for the number one time and strolling via the forest through the hungry lions and snakes and marauding adverse tribes.

Bit by using bit. You'll typically have your cave to return to. You can pick your cave.

It might be your private home, or a meditation you need, or a ordinary task you experience secure in. It doesn't rely. Even in case you're a nomad, you can still have a steady cave the usage of meditations like a guided visualisation. Or surely by means of staying on your comfort region for a while. That's first rate too. Your comfort vicinity is your warmth cushty cave and it's incredible to want to be there once in a while.

Revisiting the cave

If you're making correct progress however revel in your self regressing, don't fear. This took place to me and I counseled my therapist and he said this to me: Don't fear. You've been from your cave for a long time now. It's exceptional everyday to need to go all over again in for a bit and see what's nonetheless there. But you will probably apprehend there's not a good buy there for you anymore.

He end up right. I'd regressed to a bit of social tension and there wasn't some element there for me anymore. The anxiety, which my mind had concept was preserving me alive, no longer served me. The cave have become boring. When I stepped once more out of doors yet again, the whole lot appeared a brilliant deal better, even more so than it changed into before.

"Coming out of your comfort area is difficult in the beginning,

chaotic inside the center, and first-rate ultimately... in the end,

it shows you a whole new worldwide!"

— Manoj Arora

Default another time to self assurance

That's the problem about leaving your cave and dropping your fears. When that's long past, all that's left is the other aspect of things that were given passed proper all the way down to us too – self notion. Courage. Deep down, while we've shed the concern, we default to courageous.

So even as you want to enhance your life, that's all you've have been given to do. Leave the cave. Leave it, watching for and accepting that it's going to be a hint scary and make you a chunk worried. There are snakes in that wooded area. Except there aren't anymore, virtually.

Then as you revel in your self making progress, step out similarly and in addition. That's the way you enhance your existence and benefit self perception — with the beneficial resource of converting it for the better, although it makes you disturbing. If you all at once enjoy out of your intensity, step decrease again into the cave for a while. It'll be there for you. That's now not losing, or taking a backward step. That's what we superior to do, so bypass ahead. If it feels comfortable, stay for some time until you want to get once more outdoor. It's a cute and beneficial metaphor, and metaphors work.

You would possibly probably discover there's not whatever there in that cave for you anymore. That may be due to the fact your existence is now higher outdoor the cave. You don't need it anymore. You're defaulting over again to yourself assurance. It become there all along.

FACT

Introverts carry out well as leaders and outperform extroverted CEO's — specifically in the event that they lease extroverts to paintings for them. Introverts also paintings higher than extroverts beneath extroverted managers.

Make Networking Effective and Painless with the Awesome Combo of Coffee and Kindness

Chapter 10: A change of thinking takes the horribleness out of networking

If you hate networking, now's the time to begin changing your mind-set. Networking can be crucial.

I used to dread networking too. Really dread it. Not first-rate did I actually have social tension, however I moreover decided the entirety truly cringeworthy. There's no longer anything worse than assembly a load of strangers to peer what you may get out of them, proper?

Absolutely right.

That type of networking is horrible till you're a manifestly extroverted salesman kind. But most parents aren't. The phrase networking brings with it advantageous connotations and bags. Images of rooms complete of strangers all hoping to fulfill someone to assist them with their desires.

Fake fits chatting up one of a kind fake fits, all trying to get what they want. Yuck.

But it's good enough. Really, it's good enough. It doesn't should be like that. Ok, once in a while it's miles like that, but you may provide that sort of issue a nice extensive swerve. Go for a higher alternative. One that's warmer and tastes super and leaves everyone satisfied whether or no longer you've succeeded in locating a cutting-edge day contact or now not.

Coffee

Not see you later inside the past, there was some superb recommendation going round that during case you wanted to satisfy a person for networking motives who changed into slightly from your attain, deliver an electronic mail and provide to shop for them a espresso in exchange for a chat.

It end up right advice. It became drawing close to humans on the supply, now not the take, and it worked. It opened a few doors. I met some remarkable people this manner. But now, I've heard loads of human beings at the aspect of being presented espresso not find it impossible to resist. It's passed off too normally. It's beginning to be regarded as an offer of a $4 cup of coffee for an hour consultation well properly really worth far extra. The interpretation of the offer has modified. This makes me sad because of the truth I simply had some awesome times with some excellent humans and made some fantastic buddies. But I get it. How many strangers are you able to drink coffee with, in the long run?

If you're the use of this method, which I nevertheless love, it can now be better to apply it with people at your very very own degree in some aspect enterprise you're in. It's no longer possible to inform how the larger fish will take the provide.

There's moreover the difficulty of manipulation. Since it have become public information that studies confirmed that placing a warmness drink in people's arms is much more likely to elicit a fine, a few savvy human beings have emerge as sceptical of the espresso offerors. I don't blame them. People will try any little trick to get ahead, although it's miles as seemingly innocent as buying them a espresso. It's actually well worth noting that have a look at didn't replicate, except.

But there are although properly strategies to do it. Despite being historically shy and a person who end up the worst networker in the room, I've had been given pretty true at it. Being no longer able to do topics the ordinary manner makes you discover specific strategies to do it. I overhauled my whole view of networking, and determined one that works out properly for all of us.

Kindness

The pull away problem in networking comes from the fact you recognise you're at the take, hoping you may get what you need from different people, and that everybody is aware about what's happening. There's an time desk below every pleasantry. It's an unnatural manner to satisfy human beings and locations everybody's shield up because of the reality they comprehend humans want something from them, even though they're furthermore there in the hopes to get a few element. Horrible.

That's a few issue I'll not have any a part of. Instead, I forget about that I want some thing, and acquire that I may meet ideal people with mutual pastimes and might not, and go out with a unique cause in thoughts: kindness.

Not the type of fake kindness that entails licking someone's boots or worse. That's surely as horrible as it's furthermore manipulative. Genuine kindness. Offering true assist, with zero expectations in cross lower back. If outstanding matters come of it, extremely good. If not, I've probably had an excellent time besides. Plus I like supporting humans, so it absolutely works in particular nicely for me. If I don't meet someone who can paintings with me, I revel in giving someone else a bit nudge within the right path. But there's a few thing else I moreover like, which brings us once more to in which we started out out.

Coffee and kindness

I love espresso. In all my time within the film employer, one of the subjects I've enjoyed maximum is eating coffee with people. In evaluation, the bits I in no manner want to do all over again incorporate taking walks round a bar at a busy networking event. So now I live with coffee. And kindness.

It's tremendous to think that a part of my hobby is to take a seat down and drink espresso with human beings. I can't constantly assist them due to the fact I'm no organization hotshot and I don't have organisation money to command. But I have to make connections and introductions, and bring greater people and information to the espresso desk. Often I'll discover new people to artwork with and often I gained't. But both way, I've had espresso and been type, so it's all accurate. If it doesn't artwork, so be it. Because the opportunity way probably wouldn't have worked besides.

www.ingramcontent.com/pod-product-compliance
Lightning Source LLC
Chambersburg PA
CBHW060223030426
42335CB00014B/1321